THE GARDENER'S BUG BOOK

EARTH-SAFE INSECT CONTROL

THE GARDENER'S BUG BOOK

EARTH-SAFE INSECT CONTROL

Barbara Pleasant

Storey Publishing

The mission of Storey Publishing is to serve our customers by publishing practical information that encourages personal independence in harmony with the environment.

Edited by Elizabeth P. Stell
Cover design by Leslie Morris Noyes
Text design by Michelle Arabia
Text production by Leslie Carlson
Line drawings by Judy Eliason, except for pages 35, 37, 39 (bottom), 40, (bottom), 44, 45 (top), 47, 51, 54 (bottom), 56 (top), 59, 60, 61, 62, 65, 67, 69 (top), 70 (bottom), 74, 76, 77, 79, 84, 85, 87 (bottom), 91, 94, 95, 96 (top), and 99, which are by Cathy Baker.
Indexed by Wood-Matthews Editorial Services, Inc.

The information in this book is true and complete to the best of our knowledge. All recommendations are made without guarantee on the part of the author or Storey Publishing. The author and publisher disclaim any liability in connection with the use of this information. For additional information, please contact Storey Publishing, 210 MASS MoCA Way, North Adams, MA 01247.

Storey books are available for special premium and promotional uses and for customized editions. For further information, please call 1-800-793-9396.

Printed in the United States by Versa Press
20   19   18   17   16   15   14   13

Library of Congress Cataloging-in-Publication Data

Pleasant, Barbara.
    The gardener's bug book : earth-safe insect control/Barbara Pleasant.
       p.   cm.
    Rev. ed. of: The bug book / Helen and John Philbrick. 1974.
    Includes bibliographical references (p.   ) and index.
    ISBN 978-0-88266-609-9
    1. Insect pests – Biological control. 2. Insect pests – Control.
    3. Organic gardening. I. Philbrick, Helen Louise Porter, 1910–
    Bug book. II. Title.
SB933.3P58   1994
635'.0497—dc20
                                                  93-36907
                                                       CIP

CONTENTS

PREFACE TO THE REVISED EDITION

To try to synthesize nature's kingdom
Helen and John Philbrick
The Bug Book, 1974

Gardeners are never alone. Insects, birds, frogs, and other creatures always are present in any garden. Some are welcome companions; others look for any opportunity to nibble on treasured garden plants.

This book shares the same purpose as the original version of *The Bug Book*, first published in 1974. "To try to synthesize nature's kingdom" is the constant challenge of any gardener, for all gardens are natural environments. Since creatures large and small can become nuisances when there are too many of them, good gardeners must know when to intervene on behalf of their plants, gently and intelligently, so other forms of life that pose no threat can proceed with their small but important lives.

Entomologists, who study the lives and habits of insects, and horticulturists, who seek to understand the strengths and weaknesses of plants, have given us much information to use in understanding how our gardens fit into nature's kingdom. We now know that the same substance in a cucumber leaf that tells a spider mite it is in the wrong place may signal a cucumber beetle to call its friends — the feast is ready! Each time a scientist learns a new detail about how and why insects live, gardeners have a new piece of knowledge to fit into the puzzle that is the mosaic of life present in their garden.

When Helen and John Philbrick first wrote *The Bug Book* twenty years ago, they helped to preserve techniques and methods for harmless insect control that were in danger of being forgotten due to the seldom-questioned and intense use of broad-spectrum insecticides. But times have changed, and gardeners who are unwilling to kill every life form in order to control a single insect are now a majority.

The tremendous body of knowledge that has emerged from the modern way of thinking about nature (and the roles insects play in it) has led to the invention and discovery of new bug-control methods that are safer for gardeners and less threatening to beneficial insects and birds. I hope that you find in these pages the same clarity and usefulness thousands of gardeners have enjoyed from the Philbricks' book, plus the most up-to-date information possible on harmless insect controls.

Barbara Pleasant

◀ CHAPTER 1 ▶

INSECT CONTROL
in Your Own Backyard

*Man masters nature not by force but by understanding.
This is why science has succeeded where magic failed:
because it has looked for no spell to cast on nature.*
Jacob Bronowski
Universities Quarterly, 1956

As gardeners, our first concern is how insects live, feed, and expire on our own small pieces of land. The place where wildly exuberant insects come and go in utter freedom is the same place where we hope to grow productive vegetable gardens, fragrant and beautiful flowers, and perhaps enough fruit to sweeten up our summers. Bringing together a fair and peaceable meeting of these two worlds, of insects and gardeners, is the purpose of this book.

The best way to begin is by examining and perhaps adjusting our attitudes toward insects. It is tempting to view them as outright enemies, but this is a disservice to our intellects and to the natural ecology of which we are a part. Curiosity and respect for the fact that all living things have a place is a more fitting starting place, for our only claim to true knowledge of insects is that gained by thoughtful inquiry and experience.

When a situation with a problem insect becomes understood, our reaction should be to invoke gentle controls. Aspiring to achieve insect extinction is seldom practical and may be counterproductive as well. Extremely toxic measures that wipe out a problem insect population can easily spill over into the lives of other creatures, such as honeybees, whose presence in the garden is as welcome as our own.

Many gardeners who have been working with their soil, plants, and resident insects over a period of years notice a slow but steady decrease in pest-related garden problems. Sometimes the change occurs so slowly that we hardly notice it. Then one day we realize that a year has slipped by, and the cartons and bottles of organic pesticides, kept on a high closet shelf, have not been touched. Upon reflection, we wonder whether more wild birds are making homes on our property, gobbling up pests for breakfast, lunch, and dinner. As our gardens expand into fine-tuned collections that include more and more perennials, so does our property's potential to host more beneficial insects that need comfy places to live from year to year. And on a more basic level, it certainly must be acknowledged that better-quality soil results in healthier plants that are better able to cope with insect attacks.

Much of this book details intervention strategies for individual pests, but first several *general* principles of insect control merit careful thought and understanding. For gardeners, one of the most important ways to avoid insect problems is to choose dependable plants for the climate and season. For example, cabbage, broccoli, and their close relatives are happiest when grown in cool weather. In northern areas where cool weather is likely to prevail throughout the summer, very vigorous, high-quality brassicas are easily grown. In this situation, the plants may be bothered by a few predictable yet manageable pests. Yet if the same plants are grown in a warm climate during the hottest part of the year, their quality will be poor, and they will no doubt delight many hot-weather insects that happen to find them.

Assuming you are growing plants that are well adapted to the climate and season, the next step toward insect control is to learn about the most serious insect pests in your area and start catching and disposing of egg-laying adults before they can reproduce. Cool spring mornings can be a huge asset in these efforts, for most insects move slowly when temperatures are low. Whether you are gathering parent potato beetles or the first slugs of the season, each adult you capture may mean a hundred eggs not laid or a dozen leaves not eaten.

Most insects are summer phenomena. When autumn comes, their interests shift to finding winter shelter or secure places to hide caches of eggs, and again the gardener gets an opportunity to intervene in a passive yet important way. Turning up soil to expose hidden eggs and larvae to air, sun, rain, and cold can be a highly effective control measure. Invite birds to join you in this soil-cleaning process by luring them close with bird houses and feeders.

There is nothing new about these general approaches to insect control. They have been practiced since medieval times, and probably before, yet were forced into obscurity when highly efficient poisons made it possible for people to destroy entire communities of insects with a single squirt or spray. You can still do this, of course, but in so doing you may be tainting the environment in ways we barely understand and inviting the emergence of more sinister enemies than the one you just killed. Worst of all, you will risk turning the fun and fascination of gardening into a never-ending, unwinnable war. The plants you so desperately attempt to protect will always be rooted in the ground and will never be able to fly into the sky to do battle with moths, flies, and winged beetles. It makes more sense to assist plants on their own terms, by giving them good soil in which to grow, allowing them the companionship of friendly neighbors, and offering security from insects whose talents for destruction far exceed what seems reasonable or right.

Managing pest problems using only gentle, earth-safe methods of control does not require gardeners to lower the quality standards of the foods they grow. Rather, it involves a heightened respect for nature, a willingness to be entertained and intrigued, and increased expectations of yourself as a gardener.

◀ CHAPTER 2 ▶

GETTING TO KNOW INSECTS
Their Life Cycles, Habits,
and Interactions with Plants

*Punctually as darkness falls, our whole family goes and calls
upon her [the spider]. Big and little, we stand amazed at her
wealth of belly and her exuberant somersaults in the maze of
quivering ropes; we admire the faultless geometry of the net
as it gradually takes shape. All agleam in the lantern-light,
the work becomes a fairy orb, which seems woven of moon-
beams.*

Jean-Henri Fabre
The Life of the Spider, 1912

Living and gardening alongside insects requires that we know who
they are and understand how they live. The simplest way to identify any insect is to look at a picture. The drawings in this book
illustrate what various insects look like. Many other nature guides
and field books provide color photographs that can further help
you discern one bug from another. But be forewarned that several
common insects, including helpful lady beetles and not-so-helpful
blister beetles and cucumber beetles, come in different colors.

In addition to identifying insects with your eyes, consider
where you find them and what they are doing. Most insects are
quite particular where their food supply is concerned and will eat
only certain plants. Since very young insects have limited abilities
to move about, the adults are careful to lay eggs on or very near

plants that are suitable for their young to eat. Yet the right host plant for an egg or larva may not be the right host for the adult form of the very same insect. For example, the flamboyant caterpillar known as the parsley worm eats leaves of parsley, celery, and carrots. The adult form of the parsley worm, the black swallowtail butterfly, sips only the nectar of flowers, and her only interest in your parsley has to do with the laying of her eggs.

How do insects find their host plants? Many are able to "smell" the character of a plant with their feet or antennae, while others look for certain colors, such as the bright orange-yellow of squash blossoms. Still other insects may sample whatever plant they happen to land on and then decide whether they have found a good place to feed. By paying close attention to where insects are found, you can often easily discern their identity.

Another helpful identification factor to consider is when the insect appears. Some pests, like flea beetles, feed most heavily in early spring; others wait to appear in midsummer or even fall. The time when you first start seeing a certain species is called the emergence time, which means nothing more than the time when the insect normally emerges from wherever it has spent the preceding season and begins to feed.

Tracking emergence times of pests that appear year after year in your garden yields excellent information to use in planning a more pest-resistant garden. If your snap beans are *always* overrun by Mexican bean beetles in early July, for example, you will know to start looking for eggs just after the first of June. In many instances, you may be able to schedule plantings so that they escape damage entirely. Eggplant set out late has fewer problems with flea beetles. Corn planted early may be damaged only slightly by European corn borers. If you really want to be a good garden manager, keep records of emergence times and pest activities.

Though many people refer to all pests as "bugs," entomologists and other students of the insect world apply this name only to the true bugs, which include stink bugs, squash bugs, and tarnished plant bugs. Beetles are not bugs, but they do have the six legs that identify them as insects.

Several common garden creatures are not even insects. Spiders, pill bugs, slugs, snails, and earthworms are noninsects, but they have such strong interactive relationships with insects that we often regard them as bona fide members of the garden's insect community. In the interest of accuracy, we must acknowledge that true bugs are minor players in the insect world, and that every creature that hops, crawls, or slithers from plant to plant on more than six legs (or no legs) is not really an insect at all.

INSECT LIFE CYCLES

In addition to studying where and when various insects appear, you will need to understand what you are seeing. Insects can exhibit some pretty strange stages of growth. Relatively few garden creatures — grasshoppers, spiders, and shield bugs, for example — are born looking somewhat like miniature adults. Most others go through four stages of growth: egg, larva, pupa, and adult. How well pesky insects can be controlled during these different stages depends on the insect in question.

Moths, butterflies, beetles, flies, and many other insects have four distinct phases of development as shown in the illustration on page 8. Many hibernate through the winter as adults, but some spend the winter as eggs, larvae, or pupae.

Dragonflies, true bugs, grasshoppers, and noninsects such as spiders do not pupate. The larvae, called nymphs, often resemble the adults they are destined to become, so they have no need for the shape-changing magic of pupation. Either adults or eggs may overwinter, depending on the species and climate. Hatchlings usually emerge in mid-spring to late spring. The three-stage life cycle is shown on page 9.

The Egg Stage

Several insects lay eggs in such obvious and predictable places that a gardener can easily seek out and destroy them in the egg stage. Squash bugs are one of the best examples, for they usually

Four-Stage Metamorphosis

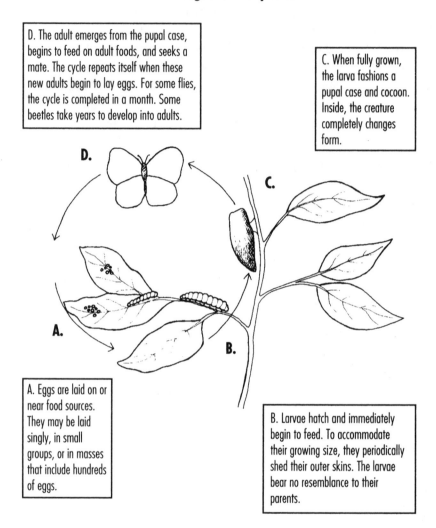

D. The adult emerges from the pupal case, begins to feed on adult foods, and seeks a mate. The cycle repeats itself when these new adults begin to lay eggs. For some flies, the cycle is completed in a month. Some beetles take years to develop into adults.

C. When fully grown, the larva fashions a pupal case and cocoon. Inside, the creature completely changes form.

A. Eggs are laid on or near food sources. They may be laid singly, in small groups, or in masses that include hundreds of eggs.

B. Larvae hatch and immediately begin to feed. To accommodate their growing size, they periodically shed their outer skins. The larvae bear no resemblance to their parents.

lay their eggs in groups on the tops of squash leaves, on or near the central leaf vein. Bright orange Colorado potato beetle eggs sometimes can be found on leaf undersides or near the potato plants' blossoming tips. Yellowish eggs found on the undersides of bush snap beans were almost certainly laid by Mexican bean beetles.

Many insects are masters at hiding their eggs. The flies whose larvae become root maggots stash their eggs in the soil around

Three-Stage Life Cycle

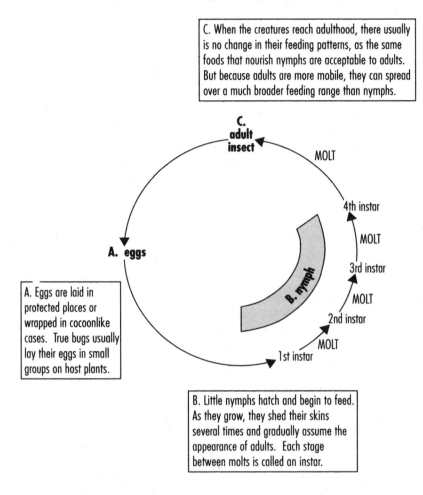

C. When the creatures reach adulthood, there usually is no change in their feeding patterns, as the same foods that nourish nymphs are acceptable to adults. But because adults are more mobile, they can spread over a much broader feeding range than nymphs.

C. adult insect

MOLT

4th instar

MOLT

A. eggs

3rd instar

MOLT

B. nymph

2nd instar

MOLT

1st instar

A. Eggs are laid in protected places or wrapped in cocoonlike cases. True bugs usually lay their eggs in small groups on host plants.

B. Little nymphs hatch and begin to feed. As they grow, they shed their skins several times and gradually assume the appearance of adults. Each stage between molts is called an instar.

plants that the larvae will want to eat. Cankerworms hide their eggs in the crevices of trees where they are nearly impossible to see. Perhaps the smartest of egg layers are beneficial insects that lay their eggs inside other insects. Braconid and ichneumon wasps use caterpillars and borers as nurseries for their young. Lady beetles find aphids and lay eggs close by, so their hatchlings won't have to travel far to find their dinner. Whenever you encounter insect eggs that you cannot immediately identify, it's a good idea to watch them daily and see what they become. If they turn out to be a destructive insect, you can easily control them if they are freshly hatched and not yet equipped to move from place to place.

The Larval Stage

Most garden insects that chew leaves, suck sap, or gobble roots do their worst damage during their larval stage. Caterpillars, root-eating maggots and grubs, and soft-bodied, monstrous looking creatures are often insect larvae. Their sole mission in life is to eat and grow so they can develop into adults. Using control methods that force the larvae to eat something that will make them sick is a prime way to intervene when pests are in their larval stage.

For a gardener, it is quite fortunate that larvae have a hard time moving about — it often makes them easy to control compared to their adult forms. For example, cabbage loopers and imported cabbageworms are easy to handpick, but the moths they become (when fully mature) are impossible to capture in great numbers. Various root maggots, as well as beetle larvae such as the northern corn rootworm, usually overwinter in the soil around host plants, so rotating the host crop frustrates the pests by robbing them of an easy food supply.

Many of the worst insect pests are larvae that feed on the plant parts we cannot see, such as roots or the insides of stems. But again, simply knowing what plant is being attacked and the mode of assault helps us identify the insect. When a whole group of plants is suffering from an apparent insect attack but you cannot see clear evidence of the culprit's identity, by all means pull or dig up a representative plant and check the insides of the roots and stems for clues.

Mysterious Metamorphoses

Following the larval stage, many insects become pupae, an intriguing stage during which they change forms completely. Most insects pupate inside protective cocoons or pupal cases, usually elongated in shape and often the same color as the soil, bark, or plant on which they are found.

Pupae are so lacking in distinctive characteristics that they are very difficult to identify. Few destructive insects can be controlled during their short and secretive pupal stage, both because they are hidden and because they are protected by their cocoon or case. Birds are able to find and consume pupae, but people can only look and wonder about this mysterious phase of insect life. When you do run across a pupa, observe it to see what happens. If the pupa is big enough for you to find, chances are good that a moth or butterfly will emerge within three weeks.

Adult Insects

Insects that are born looking somewhat like little adults gradually change size and color by molting several times. The bigger they get, the easier they are to see but the harder they are to catch. Yet catch them you must if you intend to subvert the next generation. By the time insects become adults, either by molting several times or by emerging from pupation, they are usually ready to reproduce.

The adult forms of many insects are relatively light feeders, having done much of their eating as juveniles. There are exceptions, such as the Japanese beetle, which eats voraciously as both a larva (grub) and an adult. Yet many adult pests fly fast and remain so constantly preoccupied with mating and egg laying that they eat and drink only enough to stay alive.

INSECT EATING HABITS

Identifying the good and bad insects that lurk among your garden plants is a constant source of fascination for the gardener whose goal is to grow productive plants within the framework that nature has provided. In addition to identifying insects based on their appearance, observing the behavior of those creatures will yield important clues as to possible methods of control.

Most insects that damage plants do so by eating leaves, sucking plant juices, or boring their way inside stems, trunks, or

Keeping Collectible Bugs

When you encounter insects you would like to watch closely, keep them as captives for a while. How you house the insects depends primarily on their age. In all cases, it's best to keep insects outdoors so they will remain attuned to the natural environment — and won't get loose in your house.

To observe eggs or pupae found on plants:
Tie a length of sheer fabric over the egg-bearing leaves or stem and check it daily. Or cut off leaves with eggs or pupae on them and place them in a large jar. Cover the jar with cheesecloth or another sheer fabric held in place with rubber bands. Add a handful or two of damp soil, then add a small amount of water every few days to keep the eggs or pupae from drying out.

To observe eggs, larvae, or pupae found in soil:
Excavate the eggs, larvae, or pupae, keeping as much soil intact as possible. Fill a broad jar, a small fishbowl, or an old aquarium tank one-quarter full with soil taken from the place where you found the eggs. Plant a small plug of grass or common weed in the soil. Place eggs at the same depth that you found them. Pupae may be tucked just below the soil's surface. Larvae will move to where they want to be. Sprinkle the container's interior with water to keep it slightly moist. Cover the top with cheesecloth or another sheer fabric held in place with rubber bands. If nothing has happened after three weeks of warm weather, you may have an insect that feeds below ground. Pull up the plug of grass and look for root-eating larvae.

To observe insects found feeding in the garden:
Place them in a large jar, small fishbowl, old aquarium tank, or bug box that has a lid or cover. You can use any box or enclosure that has big windows covered with polyester window-screening material, or you can buy a cricket cage wherever fishing equipment is sold.

(continued)

Along with the insects, include several sprigs of the plant on which they were feeding and enough leaf litter to cover the bottom of the enclosure. Also include a jar lid filled with water.

To save insects for mounted collections:
Saturate several cotton balls with rubbing alcohol and place them in the bottom of a jar. Cut a cardboard circle that will fit inside the jar and place it over the cotton balls. Catch the insect, using a net if the creature has fragile wings. Place it in the jar, cover, and leave it there until it is dead. Remove the insect, arrange it the way you want it, and mount it on a sewing pin stuck into a Styrofoam or other soft-textured board.

branches. Each mode of assault is accompanied by clues that can help you identify the insect that is causing the problem.

▲ **Leaf-eating insects** chew and digest large amounts of leaf and stem and invariably leave a trail of excrement behind. The presence of missing leaf parts, together with dark pebbles of digested plant material, tells you that a leaf eater is present. If the pest is well camouflaged, you may see its trail before you find the insect.

▲ **Sucking insects** feed by inserting needle-sharp mouthparts into leaves and stems. These pricks often result in tiny, puckered spots on plant leaves, usually along the leaf veins. Sucking insects often only slightly damage plants with their feeding, but they may wreak much havoc if they happen to transmit bacterial or viral diseases or appear in large numbers (as aphids sometimes do). Sudden wilting and unnatural crinkling of plant parts are the most common symptoms of such insect-vectored diseases.

▲ **Borers,** like leaf chewers, digest large amounts of plant tissue. The end product of digestion (called frass) usually accumulates outside the insect's entry hole. When borers attack woody plants, the frass is often dry, like very fine sawdust. Frass from squash borers is powdery when dry, but it may be sticky when fresh. Wipe away the frass to find the hole made by the borer.

▲ **Root feeders** literally chomp the feet out from under growing plants. Affected plants become wilted, and no amount of watering can perk them up. To identify these pests, such as cabbage or onion root maggots, pull up a damaged plant and look for the pests on the roots and in surrounding soil.

▲ **Fruit feeders** usually hatch from eggs deposited inside fruits, and the larvae feed in secret. Fruitworms and other pests that feed inside fruits and vegetables often cause heartbreaking damage since they eat the plant parts we want for ourselves. Learn the life cycles of these pests so you can intervene when they are at their most vulnerable stage of development.

GENTLE INTERVENTION

When control is called for, gardeners can choose from a steadily increasing assortment of natural, low-impact chemical controls available on store shelves, as well as the homemade concoctions and formulas described in this book. If one appreciates the necessity for preserving beneficial insects, it follows that one would choose the least toxic method that provides an acceptable level of control.

Yet not all insect control is accomplished by applied substances, either chemical or biological. Many garden insects are controlled simply by the creation of maximum biological efficiency in the plants themselves. Healthy plants may have a few insects nibbling or sucking here and there, but they are not completely devastated by them. An example appears in many gardens year after year: some flea beetles early in the season eat small holes in turnip greens and tomato leaves. But their season is short, and long before the turnips are formed in the ground or the fruits are developed on the tomato plant, the flea beetles have vanished. If the plants were not strong enough to tolerate a few small holes in their leaves, the damage would be important. But with well-nurtured plants, the damage is barely noticeable and may even strengthen the plants' defenses. Scientists now tell us that a little insect feeding may cause plants to develop chemicals in their leaves that discourage further feeding by insect pests.

Another kind of insect control suited to the small backyard garden is the use of predacious insects to prey upon those that cause trouble. In this sort of "organized mayhem," the insects that eat plants are in turn killed by other insects. Predators such as roving mantises and assassin bugs; larval lady beetles and lacewings, which eat aphids; and the parasitic braconid wasp, which makes its home in or on the bodies of tomato hornworms, are but a few examples.

In recent years, several of these predacious insects have become available for sale, but there are a few pitfalls for gardeners who hope to purchase bugs as a reliable method of insect control. The most important thing to keep in mind is that insects — no matter where they come from — must have suitable habitats and food to survive. Otherwise, they will die or move on to a place where they can live more comfortably.

Importing too many beneficial insects also may cause problems for the species that occur naturally in your yard. Ecological niches can accommodate only so many occupants, and you may risk the loss of supremely adapted indigenous species of, say, praying mantises, if you release a great number of store-bought specimens with which your natives must compete. Alternatively, if you've never seen a lacewing in your garden, attempts to establish a resident population by distributing purchased eggs will likely do no harm.

Among the gentlest pest controls is growing specific plant varieties that pests do not like. The reasons insects bypass insect-resistant varieties vary from the chemical to the physical. In the case of nonbitter cucumbers, cucumber beetles fail to find the chemical compound that signals them to feed. Some varieties of corn have a substance in their silks that discourages feeding by corn earworms. In these and other situations where the plants themselves invoke chemical defenses against pests, the gardener must understand that the result is a reduction in the feeding, reproduction, and overall vigor of the pests. Pests may still feed, but in greatly reduced numbers and with less enthusiasm.

Plants also may offer physical resistance to insect injury, which is a fascinating subject to explore in your own garden. For example, if you grow red-colored kale, kohlrabi, or cabbage, cabbageworms and cabbage loopers will lose one of their major defenses — camouflage — so both you and other predators, such as birds, can much more easily find and eliminate them. Many plants also defend themselves with leaf hairs that are sharp enough to stab small insects (such as aphids and mites on lima beans) or sticky hairs loaded with chemicals that make insects sick (tomatoes and potatoes have these). Still other vegetables slow down the proliferation of insects by making them ingest so much plant fiber that they expend too much energy eating. In this way, southern peas (cowpeas) with thick pod walls discourage curculios, tomatoes with thick skins and dense flesh frustrate fruitworms, and ears of corn with thick, tight husks prove problematic for corn earworms.

DECIDING WHAT TO DO

By the time you have identified a problem insect in your garden, you will know quite a bit about the nature of its tactics. Successfully intervening to protect plants from further injury calls for thinking through these clues. For example, an insect that eats leaves may be managed by coating its dinner with a substance that deters further feeding. In contrast, an insect that uses a hit-and-run sucking strategy is better managed by other methods, such as companion planting (to make the culprit's preferred food plants harder to find), exclusion with row floating covers, or use of resistant plants.

In brief, controlling garden pests is often a five-step process:

1. Take a captive and try to identify it. Place the insect in a glass or clear plastic jar and study it with a magnifying glass. Place a leaf of the suspected food plant in the jar and see if the bug continues to feed.

2. Go back to the plant and look for more evidence of how the insect launched its attack. Check for hidden eggs. Look at other plants that are closely related to the damaged ones and see if they show evidence of insect feeding.

3. Check the list in the next chapter, "Common Food Plants and the Pests That Love Them," and see if you can find your insect.

4. Look up your prime suspect in Chapter 4, "Common Garden Insects: Identification and Control," and decide on a gentle yet specific way to keep it under control.

5. Wait a couple of days, then evaluate your efforts. If damage continues unabated, try a second method of control or sacrifice the most infested plants to curtail more widespread problems.

The Company They Keep

Companion plants are an ecological angle to exploit in your efforts to create a well-balanced garden environment. These are plants that may confuse insect pests, repel them, or serve as protected havens for beneficial insects.

You may use these suggested companion plants as a starting point, but effective companion planting is something that must be learned through experience in *your own garden*. The assortment of insects present in your garden is not like that in any other, so the relationships that exist or develop between the plants and insects in your yard are unique by nature.

When experimenting with new or different companion plants, keep in mind these common characteristics of good companions:

▲ **Noncompetitive.** The best companion plants provide the right amount of shade and shelter in relation to the needs of their neighbors, and below ground they do not aggressively claim the root zone all to themselves. Good examples include radishes in and around summer squash and onions among cabbage-family crops.

▲ **Pollen producers.** Many beneficial insects are attracted to plants that produce a lot of pollen. Flowers that drop pollen on tabletops after they are cut and arranged in vases often attract honeybees, tiny wasps, and other helpful insects. Heavy pollen producers include tansy, corn, and many ornamentals and wildflowers.

▲ **Nice noses.** Fragrant flowers and aromatic herbs may repel or confound insects that use their olfactory senses to locate food plants. Mints, basils, fennel, garlic and other aromatic herbs, marigolds, nasturtiums, and other flowers can fill this niche.

▲ **Longevity.** Many large beneficial insects and spiders need habitats that stay put all summer, or better yet, perennial plants that come back year after year. Examples include rosemary, horseradish, and cover crops such as clovers, grains, and soybeans.

The original *Bug Book* listed specific companion plants for many vegetables, but scientific inquiry into the effects of companion planting combinations during the past twenty years has been inconclusive. However, the characteristics of good companion plants (as described above) are widely held to be valid, especially since they can be incorporated into existing or specific planting schemes to suit distinctive garden situations. In other words, companion planting is not so much about plopping down the "right" plants next to each other as it is about strengthening the relationships between garden plants so that they benefit one another. When you experiment with and discover plant groupings that seem to result in fewer insect pests than usual, you are one step closer to creating the healthiest, most diversified garden possible.

YOUR ROLE AS GARDEN STEWARD

Every garden method you use that helps keep plants happy, from enriching your soil to staking your peas, contributes to the defensive capabilities of your garden where insects are concerned. Approaches that directly regulate insect populations, such as handpicking pests, encouraging natural predators, and pursuing companionable relationships between plants, also help tilt the ecological scales in your favor.

Yet even as we study the life forms in our gardens in hopes of establishing plant communities that are unattractive to pests, we must recognize that it's not a war we are preparing for; rather, it's a slow evolution made up of small and large links in a natural food chain. A small change in the natural sequence of events may alter thousands of insect lives, as when a pair of bats move into a nearby tree and eliminate a million mosquitoes, night-flying beetles, and moths in the course of one summer. Similarly, one sickly squash vine, overrun with cucumber beetles and left unattended, may portend terrible devastation for fall pumpkins.

The insects in our gardens always offer new things to think about and new dramas to watch as their dog-eat-dog world is played out in miniature before our eyes. To be successful gardeners, we must take time to admire insects for their skill and determination but always be ready to assert ourselves as attentive stewards of the gardens we create.

CHAPTER 3

COMMON FOOD PLANTS
and the Pests That Love Them

This alphabetical directory of popular vegetables and fruits is intended as a quick guide to help you identify common insect pests. If the insect name appears in bold print, detailed information on its life cycle and control measures is given in Chapter 4.

VEGETABLES

Artichoke, Globe

Aphids sometimes feed on leaves.

Artichoke, Jerusalem

Insect problems are rare.

Asparagus

Asparagus beetles eat leaves and may make small brown scars on spears. Plants that grow poorly or wilt in hot weather may be infested with **symphylans. Cutworms** occasionally chew down young spears.

Basil

Young seedlings may be felled by **cutworms.** Basil normally has few problems with insects, though small beetles and caterpillars may consume a few leaves in summer.

Beans

A few days after seeds sprout, **cutworms** may topple plants by chewing just above the soil line. Potato **leafhoppers** cause leaf tips and edges to turn brown and curl under. **Mexican bean beetle** larvae rasp at leaf undersides, giving them a skeletonized appearance. Large holes in leaves may be the work of **Japanese beetles. June beetles,** cutworms, other caterpillars, and **slugs** that feed at night can cause similar damage. Holes in stored dry beans are the work of bean **weevils.** Other occasional pests include **aphids, spider mites,** and **flea beetles.** The hooked leaf hairs of lima beans usually protect them from these small insects.

Beet

Puckery yellow patches on leaves may be caused by **aphids** feeding on leaf undersides. Spinach **leaf miners** leave light-colored meandering trails and patches in older leaves. **Flea beetles** make numerous pinholes in leaves, mostly in late spring. In midsummer, **blister beetles** may begin eating beet leaves quite suddenly. **Armyworms** may find and consume fall plantings. The beet **leafhopper** spreads curly top virus, recognized by unnatural deep crinkling of new leaves.

Broccoli

Most cabbage pests will attack broccoli, including **aphids, cabbageworms, cabbage loopers, cabbage root maggots, flea beetles,** and **cutworms.** See cabbage entry below for symptoms.

Brussels Sprouts

Same as cabbage.

Cabbage

Cabbageworms and **cabbage loopers** are both small green caterpillars that eat leaves and hide on leaf veins. The **cabbage root maggot** feeds on cabbage roots in late spring, killing young seedlings. **Cutworms** may fell unprotected cabbage seedlings shortly after they are set out. **Flea beetles** usually damage plants only slightly. In areas where cabbage remains in the ground in midsummer, **harlequin bugs** and other shield bugs may damage it. **Slugs** like the shelter of large cabbage plants and cut numerous holes in outer leaves. Where **symphylans** are present in the Northwest, young plants may be stunted or killed.

Carrot

Aphids may feed lightly on carrot tops or roots, causing curled leaves and slow growth. Larvae of the **carrot rust fly** tunnel into roots, leaving behind orange cavities. Hungry **parsley worms** can suddenly consume carrot tops in abundance. **Tarnished plant bugs** lurk among leaves and leave dark spots where they feed. **Root-knot nematodes** cause roots to be misshapen, with round galls on small feeder roots. **Wireworms** may tunnel into mature carrots stored in the ground. **Slugs** can mysteriously thin out small seedlings.

Cauliflower

The pest list is the same as for cabbage, although problems are usually limited to **cabbageworms, cabbage loopers,** and **aphids** when fast-maturing varieties are grown.

Celeriac

Normally free of pests unless **parsley worms** manage to find the plants.

Celery

Sometimes **leafhoppers** and small **caterpillars** feed on celery, but the most common pests are **parsley worms,** which devour celery leaves, and **tarnished plant bugs,** which cause brown patches to form on leaves and stems where they feed.

Chicory

Very few pest problems other than a few **aphids.**

Chinese Cabbage

Aphids may become so numerous that they need to be controlled. **Flea beetles** sometimes leave tiny holes in the outer leaves of spring plantings. In warm weather, **slugs** may hide between leaves, eating holes in leaves and small cavities in the ribs. Grow this crop quickly and keep plants widely spaced to avoid pest problems.

Chives

Very few pests except for the rare appearance of onion **thrips.**

Collards

The same pests as for cabbage, although collards are more pest resistant than other cabbage relatives. Watch for **cabbageworms** on young plants started in late summer. In early spring, **aphids** often appear in large numbers on mature plants that have stood through the winter.

Corn

Until corn is two weeks old, plants may be felled by **cutworms.** A scattering of small holes on the outer leaves may be from **flea beetles. Japanese beetles** feed on silks, tassels, and leaves in midsummer. **Corn earworms** eat silks and kernels near the tips of ears and often leave messy deposits of frass in their wake. **Corn borers** (European and other borer species) bore into stalks and ears to consume clusters of kernels. Rootworms (including the larvae of spotted **cucumber beetles)** and **wireworms** eat corn roots. Dent corn, used for meal and animal feed, is more pest resistant than sweet corn.

Cucumber

This crop is tremendously troubled by **cucumber beetles,** which feed heavily on the plants and transmit bacterial wilt. **Cutworms** may kill young seedlings. **Squash bugs** can damage plants early but usually will forsake cucumbers for squash when given the chance.

Dill

Parsley worms like to eat leaves but rarely cause problems unless they outnumber the dill plants. Most other pests stay away, possibly because the flowers are highly attractive to numerous small beneficial insects.

Eggplant

Notoriously well loved by **flea beetles,** eggplant leaves may be heavily consumed in late spring. **Colorado potato beetle** larvae often prefer eggplant leaves to potatoes early in the season, and some night-flying beetles (including **Asiatic garden beetles)** may occasionally chew large, ragged holes. **Cutworms** may girdle early transplants.

Endive

Very few pests other than **aphids** and **slugs.**

Fennel

The herb form of fennel attracts beneficial insects but occasionally has its leaves eaten by **parsley worms.** Vegetable or bulb fennel may host **slugs.**

Garlic

Very few pest problems other than the rare appearance of **onion maggots.**

Horseradish

Very few pests; may deter soil-dwelling insects.

Kale

The same pests that bother cabbage can be attracted to kale, although feeding is usually light. In early spring, **aphids** can become severe problems on plants that have overwintered.

Kohlrabi

Cabbageworms and **cabbage loopers** chew holes in kohlrabi leaves and hide on leaf veins. Other cabbage pests can attack kohlrabi, but the open growth habit of kohlrabi plants helps them resist many pest problems.

Leek

Few pests problems other than **onion maggots,** which eat small roots and cause plants to lose vigor and wilt. Onion **thrips** may leave pale patches on young leek leaves.

Lettuce

Aphids frequently lurk among lettuce leaves, but they are often controlled by lady beetles and other predators. Watch for **slugs** in wet weather.

Melons

Melons are susceptible to all cucumber pests. The worst ones usually are **cucumber beetles.** They weaken plants and transmit bacterial wilt, which causes severe daytime wilting that becomes worse over a period of a week. **Squash bugs** usually prefer squash but can become a nuisance on melons. **Spider mites** are a leading melon pest in arid climates, causing leaves to appear light and parched. Watermelons are much more pest resistant than muskmelons and honeydews.

Mustard

Few pest problems other than a few **aphids** or **flea beetles.**

New Zealand Spinach

Few pest problems other than occasional light feeding by wandering **caterpillars** and **beetles.**

Okra

Nematodes seriously distort roots and weaken plants grown in infested soil. **Asiatic garden beetles, June beetles,** or **Japanese beetles** may chew large holes in leaves. Fire **ants** have been observed eating okra flowers.

Onion

Onions grown from direct-sown seeds are sometimes bothered by **cutworms. Onion maggots** cause young plants to wilt and older ones to develop unsound bulbs. **Thrips** leave pale patches on leaves.

Parsley

The **parsley worm** eats leaves, and various soil-dwelling grubs and borers may occasionally trouble the tough roots. Let some parsley plants flower to attract beneficial insects.

Parsnip

All carrot pests can strike parsnips, although they usually don't because parsnips mature in cold weather, when few insects are active.

Peanut

Insect invasions are rare.

Pea, Southern (Cowpea)

Spider mites can become a problem in hot weather. **Ants** often shepherd small **aphid** colonies on blossoming plants. A species of curculio **(weevil)** bores into pods; other bean **weevils** also feed in dry peas grown in the East. Large paper **wasps** feed heavily on pests found on this crop.

Peas

Sweet shell peas and edible-podded peas may be bothered by **aphids,** which feed lightly but can transmit viruses. Potato **leafhoppers** and **tarnished plant bugs** leave brown spots on leaves where they feed. With leafhoppers, leaf edges often curl downward. Bean **weevils** can lurk inside dry peas.

Peppers

Insects don't seem to care if peppers are hot or sweet. **Cutworms** chew down young plants. **Aphids** and **leafhoppers** feed lightly but may transmit viral diseases. Occasionally, **blister beetles,** tomato **hornworms,** and other large **caterpillars** devour pepper leaves.

Potato

Early in the season, **flea beetles** leave tiny holes in potato leaves. If leaves have brown tips and the leaf margins begin to curl downward, look for tiny potato **leafhoppers** on leaf undersides. Just as potatoes begin growing well, **Colorado potato beetles** appear. Adults and larvae consume leaves in clearly conspicuous places, but tiny larvae may be hiding in growing tips. **Blister beetles** occasionally eat potato leaves. Misshapen potato tubers with swollen galls on them indicate the presence of root-knot **nematodes** (or some other nematode). Wandering tunnels in mature potatoes often are the work of **wireworms.**

Potato, Sweet

Flea beetles may leave tiny holes in leaves, and larvae may feed on roots. Where root-knot **nematodes** are very severe, tubers may become cracked and warted. Various **caterpillars** sometimes feed lightly on sweet potato leaves. Underground, **grubs, wireworms,** or **weevils** may make shallow holes in roots. Several modern varieties resist weevils and other insect pests.

Pumpkin

This crop suffers from both cucumber and squash pests. The most common ones are **squash bugs,** which suck stem juices and destroy the centers of leaves. Find them under stems or beneath leaves that lie close to the ground. Eggs are laid on the tops of older leaves. **Squash vine borers** can cause severe damage. Look for a weak section of stem that exudes frass, beyond which the vine wilts badly on hot days.

Radish

Flea beetles often feed lightly on spring radishes, although the plants usually grow well despite little flea-beetle holes in their leaves. Later, **harlequin bugs** may eat some leaves. **Cabbage root maggots** are serious pests. Radishes seem to repel many pests, and the flowers attract beneficial insects.

Rhubarb

Normally rhubarb is free of pests; those that do bother it inflict minimal damage. **Leafhoppers** may cause leaves to yellow a bit and curl on the edges. Various **caterpillars, slugs, Japanese beetles, and Asiatic garden beetles** may feed lightly on rhubarb leaves.

Rutabaga

Except for brief appearances by **flea beetles** and **aphids,** few pests bother this crop. However, any of the cabbage pests can feed on rutabagas in unusual years.

Salsify

This slow-growing but stalwart crop has few pest problems.

Spinach

Aphids can transmit viruses that cause new leaves to become pale, stunted, and unusually crinkled. **Leaf miners** leave light meandering trails and patches in spinach leaves. **Flea beetles** may make tiny pinholes in leaves. Leaves with large sections chewed away have probably been attacked by roving **caterpillars.**

Squash, Summer

Squash is the favorite host plant of **squash bugs,** which hide beneath leaves and stems and lay eggs on the topmost leaves. In mixed plantings, some varieties attract more squash bugs than others. **Cucumber beetles** feed on flowers and stems but seldom cripple plants. **Squash vine borers** weaken basal stems from the inside; look for holes surrounded with frass in the main stem, a few inches from the ground. **Aphids** spread viral diseases, as do some **whiteflies.** Leaves of infected plants are small and oddly crinkled and do not grow well. In hot weather, **spider mites** may cause leaves to appear pale and bleached.

Squash, Winter

The same pests that like summer squash will attack winter squash, especially **squash bugs.** Fortunately, **Squash vine borers** are usually less severe on winter squash and seldom bother butternut varieties.

Sunflower

Sunflowers are rarely the scene of insect attacks, although nocturnal **caterpillars** and beetles may leave mysterious holes in leaves. Rarely, **borers** make holes in the main stems.

Swiss Chard

The same pests that attack beets sometimes bother chard, including **leaf miners, flea beetles,** and beet **leafhoppers.** In addition, **grasshoppers** may eat chard grown in summer.

Tomato

Tomato seedlings are at high risk for **cutworm** damage. **Flea beetles** may leave small holes in leaves, but damage is usually light. **Colorado potato beetles,** especially the adults, occasionally feed on tomatoes. Missing leaves and telltale excrement usually indicate the presence of tomato **hornworms. Blister beetles** also eat leaves and appear suddenly in midsummer. Root-knot **nematodes** cause galls to form on roots of nonresistant varieties; affected plants wilt badly on hot days. Various **fruit flies** may bore into fruits just as they begin to ripen. **Slugs** eat holes in fruits and leave a shiny trail that links them to the damage. In the South, tomato fruitworms, more commonly known as **corn earworms,** also may eat fruits. **Spider mites** may cause leaves to turn pale and dry up, especially in arid climates. In warm climates, **leafhoppers** can transmit curly top virus, in which new growth is crinkled and often has brown spots. **Thrips** spread tomato spotted wilt virus, in which the topmost leaf tips show black spots followed by severe wilting. Although the list of possible tomato pests is quite long, most gardeners see only one or two of these pests in a given summer.

Turnip

Flea beetles make small holes in leaves, and **aphids** sometimes feed lightly on turnip plants. **Cabbage root maggots** may eat the roots, especially in spring. Turnip pests are usually few and sparse.

FRUITS

Apple

Codling moth larvae tunnel into little green apples through the blossom (bottom) end, causing many to drop prematurely. Infested mature fruits have brown tunnels in their cores. Curculios (such as **plum curculio**) leave crescent-shaped scars on fruits. Most inchworms feeding on apple leaves are **cankerworms. Aphids** feed on young leaves, causing them to crinkle and curl. **Scale** insects may infest individual branches, weakening their growth. **Spider mites** make leaves turn pale and dry up in midsummer. **Tent caterpillars** may establish webby colonies in limb crotches. Small white maggots feeding in fruits are **fruit fly** larvae; these may cause fruit to rot.

Apricot

The same pests that bother peaches bother apricots, including **plum curculios, Asiatic garden beetles,** and various **borers** that cause the tips of young twigs to wilt and die.

Blackberry

These brambles usually thrive in spite of visits from **aphids** and occasional stem **borers,** unless the aphids infect the plants with viruses. **Japanese beetles** and other pests of the rose sometimes defoliate blackberries. Pruning old canes to the ground after they have finished bearing limits pest problems.

Blueberry

Northern-grown blueberries may be stricken with fruit maggots (a **fruit fly**'s larvae) or fruitworms (the larvae of several small moths) that feed inside fruits. Natural predators usually keep these pests under control. Where **Japanese beetles** are numerous, they may skeletonize blueberry leaves in midsummer.

Cherry

Tent caterpillars love cherry trees and often establish colonies in the crotches between branches. These caterpillars eat leaves. **Plum curculios** make dimples and crescent-shaped scars in fruits. Very small white maggots feeding inside fruits are the larvae of a **fruit fly. Aphids** may distort young leaves when infestations are severe. **Scale** insects accumulate on individual branches, often killing them with their concentrated feeding.

Citrus

Small white cottony blobs on leaves and small stems are **mealy-bugs.** Several species of **mites** so small they can hardly be seen cause tiny yellow dots on citrus leaves; badly damaged leaves may fall to the ground. A **leaf roller** caterpillar called the navel orangeworm (larva of a light gray moth) sometimes feeds inside cracked or damaged fruit. **Aphids** are often active on citrus fruits during the winter months. Several species of **scale** and a **whitefly** may appear on all citrus fruits.

Currant

Aphids sometimes gather on leaf undersides. Several small **caterpillars** eat currant leaves. Rarely, **borers** infest old canes that should be pruned out. Little **fruit fly** maggots occasionally feed inside fruits.

Elderberry

This native fruit rarely interests pesky insects.

Fig

Cultivars that have closed eyes at the ends of the fruits are usually free of pests. In the West, little beetles called sour fruit bugs crawl inside open fig "eyes" and lay eggs. The larvae feed inside. In other areas, **ants** sometimes feed on the syrupy interior of open-eyed figs.

Gooseberry

Insect pests include all those that may damage currants, to which gooseberries are closely related.

Grape

Several small **caterpillars,** including **leaf-roller** types, feed on grape leaves. Paper **wasps** and other natural predators help to keep them under control. **Japanese beetles** eat grape leaves enthusiastically. **Mealybugs** and **whiteflies** are common grape pests in the West. In the East, a small moth lays eggs among ripening grapes, and the larvae (half-inch-long caterpillars) eat individual fruits. **Leafhoppers** occasionally feed so heavily that leaves shrivel, starting at the outside edges.

Kiwi

This unusual fruit is a great favorite of **Japanese beetles.**

Peach and Nectarine

In spring, peach **borers** feed inside the trunk and branches. **Plum curculios** blemish green and ripening fruits by making punctures and crescent-shaped wounds. Several flying beetles feed on ripe and fallen fruits. Most peach problems can be traced to diseases rather than insects.

Pear

The same **codling moths** that infest apples sometimes feed on pears, entering fruits from the blossom end. **Plum curculios** occasionally puncture fruits but are deterred by the firm flesh they encounter. A very small insect called the **pear psylla** sucks juices from leaves and fruits and leaves behind a sticky honeydew that becomes black mold.

Plum

Plums have the same problems as peaches, although they are less severe and most often limited to **plum curculios.**

Quince

Generally tougher than apples, the quince's most common pest is the **codling moth,** whose larvae burrow into young fruits.

Raspberry

Raspberry cane borers form galls on canes as they feed inside. **Grasshoppers, rose chafers,** and other rose pests may eat raspberry leaves from time to time. **Japanese beetles** skeletonize raspberry leaves. **Spider mites** can infest raspberries under hot, dry conditions. **Aphids** can transmit viruses if there are diseased plants within range.

Strawberry

Deformed fruits that ripen unevenly can be caused by pollination or weather problems, or they may be the work of **tarnished plant bugs.** Small **leaf-roller** caterpillars may feed on strawberry leaves. Clean holes found in strawberries are usually the work of **slugs** or **snails,** which love this crop.

◄ CHAPTER 4 ►

COMMON GARDEN INSECTS
Identification and Control

When a bee finds a good source of honey somewhere, after her return home she makes this known to the others in a remarkable way. Full of joy, she waltzes around among them in circles, without doubt in order that they shall notice the smell of the honey which has attached itself to her; then when she goes out again they soon follow her in crowds.

M. J. E. Spitzner
a pioneering German entomologist, 1788

The descriptions in this chapter are intended to help you identify and understand the insects you encounter in your garden. Get to know the good ones so you don't kill them by mistake. Methods for controlling those that cause problems are given, along with tips for encouraging helpful insects. Most of the control measures are explored in more depth in Chapter 5, "Remedies, Recipes, and Formulas for Earth-Safe Insect Control."

Ants

Most ants do little damage in the garden, although some ants (especially fire ants) are an unwelcome presence, particularly where children are likely to be. Some large nonbiting ants form an alliance with

adult: size varies

plant-sucking aphids, with the aphids feeding on plants while the ants consume the aphids' sticky-sweet secretions. For these ants, tolerance may be practical, or you can make a bait by mixing 1 tablespoon of boric acid with ½ cup of fruit jelly. Drop teaspoons of the mixture in jar lids or paper cupcake liners, and place the baits where the ants can find them. Warn children that these baits are poison.

To get rid of fire ants, chemical growth regulators now on the market work slowly but surely if your property is dotted with many mounds. If only a few colonies are present, try pouring a large pot of boiling water down the entry hole to each nest and repeat as necessary until the survivors move on to a less threatening homesite. Boiling water is the least toxic way to get rid of aggressive red ants in yards and gardens.

Aphids

The common name for the many species of aphids that inhabit gardens is plant lice, for that is exactly what they look like. Some species, such as cabbage aphids, are large enough to identify quickly; others are so small you need a magnifying glass to get a good look at them. But anytime you see groups of very tiny insects hanging on to a plant, they are likely to be aphids.

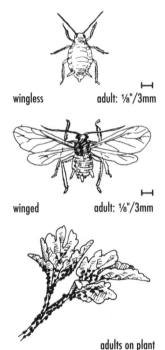

wingless   adult: ⅛"/3mm

winged   adult: ⅛"/3mm

adults on plant

Aphids suck plant juices, weakening the leaves and stems. Some also transmit plant viruses. Fortunately, there are a dozen major predators for every aphid. The most common of these predators are lady beetle larvae, small wasps, syrphid fly larvae, and lacewings.

The first thing to do when you notice the presence of aphids is to stop and think. In early spring, if they gather on flower buds of overwintered collards and kale, why not just snap off the whole gaggle and dispose of them? Most years, I see a number of reddish aphids on iris leaves, but they disappear like magic after a few weeks. By early summer, the presence of large numbers of lady beetles means that aphids are about, too.

Most of the time, you do not need an insecticide to get rid of aphids. A strong spray of water from a hose will do, as will soapy water. Or you can use insecticidal soaps made just for this purpose. These soaps contain large concentrations of fatty acids that are lethal to aphids.

All aphids have winged and nonwinged forms; the winged ones may move from one plant to another spreading plant viruses, especially in midsummer. Because they are mobile, they are very difficult to control. If they are a problem in your garden, the best approach is to use floating row covers to protect threatened plants. The garden disease most likely to be transmitted by aphids is cucumber mosaic virus (CMV; it affects many crops, especially cucumbers and spinach). Use resistant varieties if CMV is known to be common in your area.

On fruit trees, aphid eggs can be suppressed by spraying with dormant oil twice — once in late fall and again in early spring. Insecticidal soaps are safe to use against aphids on most fruits.

Armyworms

The armyworm is so named because it is known to travel like an army, en masse, devouring everything in its path. Fortunately, this happens only in rare years, particularly when damp spring weather prevails in the South. Such weather contributes to the health and vitality of the first-generation adult moths, which may

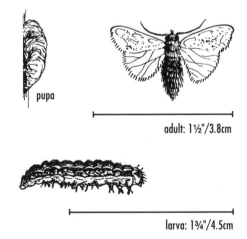

pupa

adult: 1½"/3.8cm

larva: 1¾"/4.5cm

fly hundreds of miles northward, always under cover of darkness, before settling down to lay eggs. When large numbers of eggs hatch and the caterpillars begin to feed, you have an invasion of armyworms.

Two major species are sometimes found in gardens. The true armyworm grows into a caterpillar up to two inches long, which usually starts out light green and becomes darker as it matures. It has thin white stripes down its body. True armyworms feed almost exclusively on grains and grasses and will eat other garden crops only when threatened with starvation. They feed at night and hide just below the soil's surface during the day.

The second common species, called the fall armyworm, looks very similar to the true armyworm but has a white Y pattern on its head. The fall armyworm feeds both day and night and is much more general in its food preferences, enjoying a varied diet of corn, cucumbers, tomatoes, cabbage, and all types of grains and legumes. Fall armyworms gradually move northward as the growing season progresses but may be seen quite early in the summer in southern and central regions.

In a small garden, you can handpick armyworms at night, using a flashlight to help you find them. Bt (*Bacillus thuringiensis*) usually controls severe outbreaks of either species provided you treat the infested plants early, quite soon after the worms have begun to feed.

If you have a sizable field of corn or other grain to protect and the worms are infiltrating rapidly, try this old remedy. Dig a deep, narrow trench along the sides of the field, then drag a log or other heavy object through the trench to pulverize the soil at the bottom. This makes it more difficult for the worms to get a firm foothold. Every morning, drag the trench to squash the worms that have been detained.

Both types of armyworms tend to disappear quite suddenly, as the caterpillars go underground to pupate. When the adult moths emerge two to three weeks later, they immediately take off, usually in a northerly direction.

In years when you see only a few armyworms here and there, you may decide to leave them alone. Armyworms help support numerous beneficial insects, including ground beetles, which eat them, and parasitic flies and wasps, which lay their eggs on unsuspecting armyworms.

Asiatic Garden Beetles

adult: ⅜"/10mm

An insect that has spread rapidly over the eastern two-thirds of North America since its first appearance in New Jersey in 1922, the Asiatic garden beetle looks much like a small June beetle. The adults are less than half an inch long, brown, and attracted to porch lights on summer nights, just like June beetles. Asiatic garden beetles feed at night, chewing irregular holes in many different plants, including most vegetables and many popular ornamentals. During the day, they rest in the soil.

Identify these beetles at night, either with a flashlight or by setting a light trap in the garden. Handpick them if they are few, or use a light trap if large numbers of the beetles appear.

As larvae, the small white grubs stay six inches or more below the soil's surface, so repeated tillage in the fall may help limit problems the following year. However, since the grubs are most numerous beneath weeds and grasses and the adults fly freely in search of food plants, attempts to poison this pest at either stage are unwise.

Asparagus Beetles

adult: ¼"/6mm

If you grow asparagus, resident populations of this little orange-and-black beetle may establish a comfortable home in your yard. Adults appear in spring and promptly start chewing tender asparagus spears and laying shiny black eggs. Within weeks, the eggs hatch and the larvae start feeding. Then the larvae go underground to pupate into adults. By fall, several generations may have matured, each one larger and hungrier than the one before, and you may have a real problem.

Because the beetles are small and fast, they are difficult to handpick, but it can be done in the cool of the morning, especially in early summer when asparagus foliage is sparse. Many birds will eat the beetles, so it's a good idea to lure wild birds to the area with perches in and around the asparagus bed.

Try to do a good job of asparagus beetle control in late summer so there will be fewer to tangle with the following year. Treat heavy infestations with pyrethrin or rotenone, and cut foliage off at the ground as soon as it begins to die back. Allow birds to clean up beds before applying a new layer of rich mulch in early winter.

Assassin Bugs

Sometimes called kissing bugs because they seem to kiss their prey, these predatory insects are welcome in gardens as long as you are willing to leave them alone. Like other true bugs, assassin bugs have flat bodies and wings that are usually kept folded. One unusual species called the wheel bug has a projection on its back that looks like

adult: ½" – 1"/1.3cm – 2.5cm

the cog of a wheel. All assassin bugs have longer legs than destructive bugs, such as squash bugs and stink bugs.

Typically, assassin bugs post themselves quietly at good observation points among plants and wait for an insect to pass in their range. Then they grab their prey and promptly start eating it. Be careful around assassin bugs, as they will bite you if they feel they must. Itchy bites often attributed to spiders may be the work of assassin bugs. Before reaching into plants to harvest vegetables, a good shake of the foliage will send these bugs into hiding.

Blister Beetles

Here is an insect that has the dubious honor of being both a valuable beneficial and a horrible pest. The larvae feed on grasshopper eggs, but the adults feed on tomatoes, chard, and many other vegetables and flowers.

adult: ¾"/1.9cm

In early summer to midsummer, the first you will see of blister beetles are what they leave behind: pebbly black trails of excrement. Gently shake the plant being eaten, and the striped black beetles will drop to the ground or run for cover beneath the leaves. Collect them with a gloved hand, as squashed specimens may raise a blister on your skin. In the South, where blister beetles often appear in large numbers on tomatoes, some gardeners use small hand-held vacuum cleaners to collect them. Personally, I shake them down or capture them loosely in my hand, then squash them with my foot.

The oldest remedy, used when blister beetles appear in hordes, is to drive them out of the garden with cedar or pine branches — a slow process that requires the participation of several people. If you'd rather poison them, rotenone or sabadilla will do the trick.

Borers

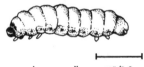

larva: usually over ½"/1.3cm

Last year some neighbors asked me what was going on with their wisterias. It was early spring, and suddenly many thin, beige wormlike things appeared sticking out from the woody parts of the plants. I touched one, and it crumbled like fine sawdust. Borers. The pest was hidden inside the wood, but we knew from the frass that borers were at work.

Hundreds of different plants get borers, and there are thousands of different kinds of borers. Peach tree and dogwood borers are well known. Squash vine borers and corn borers have their own entries in this chapter. Some borers enter through injuries in plant bark, and others hatch from eggs laid on the plant's exterior. They immediately start boring. Borers do nothing but bore, eating a diet rich in cellulose, until they mature. Most become moths.

Should a mysterious borer like the one that found my neighbors' wisterias show up in your yard, think carefully how to intervene. If the entry hole is large enough, perhaps you can wipe away the frass and impale the borer on a thin piece of wire, such as a bent-out paper clip. Syringes filled with liquid Bt are another possibility. Where borer holes are tiny and numerous, spraying high-pressure water to irrigate the holes may have some impact. Trimming off isolated branches that show borer damage is another option. The problem with poisons, even natural ones, is getting them on a pest that may be so tightly lodged within the plant that it forms a living plug in its own hole.

Braconid Wasps

adult laying eggs in aphid

adult: ⅛" – ½"/3mm – 1.3cm

Various species of this miniature wasp are among the most widely distributed beneficial insects, occurring throughout North America. The adults usually feed delicately on nectar without really damaging flowers and are attracted to plants that bear many small flowers, including dill, parsley, Queen Anne's lace, daisies, clovers, and melampodium. Although less than half an inch long, the largest species may frequently be seen visiting flowers. Look for darkly colored dwarf wasps with conspicuous exposed ovipositors, which may appear to the timid bug-watcher to be stingers.

Stingers they are, but people aren't their target. The braconid sinks her ovipositor into soft-bodied caterpillars and borers, where the eggs hatch and feed inside the host. Some species complete their life cycles inside the host, whereas others spin cocoons attached to the outside of the caterpillar. Gardeners frequently encounter tomato hornworms bearing these cocoons. When you happen upon one of these braconid nurseries but do not wish to tolerate its host's continued feeding on your garden plants, keep it in a jar until the wasps emerge and then release them.

Other evidence that braconids are at work include colonies of aphids that are all dead, with tiny holes in their bodies. The braconid responsible for such aphid massacres is much smaller than the one that parasitizes hornworms and is rarely seen. She wisely deposits only one egg in each aphid, so a single braconid mother may be responsible for the slow death of hundreds of aphids.

Braconid wasps may be purchased and introduced into a garden, although you will likely attract a teeming population by simply growing the plants they like. Braconids often emerge quite early in the season, as they spend their winters hidden inside hosts hibernating below ground.

Cabbage Loopers

See **Cabbageworms.**

Cabbage Root Maggots

adult: ⅓"/9mm

When seedlings of cabbage and cabbage cousins suddenly wilt and die within weeks after they are set out, the culprit may be cabbage root maggots, the larvae of a small fly. Pull up a recent casualty and look for the one-quarter-inch-long legless white maggots. These larvae burrow into the stem, just below the ground, and feed on the stem and roots. If they do not kill the seedlings, they weaken them badly and create numerous entry points for disease organisms. Damaged plants rarely produce well.

To keep a resident population from becoming established, pull up all cabbage-family plants following harvest and destroy them rather than turning them under. Rotate plantings to reduce repeat infestations and to shortcut the buildup of soilborne diseases that often follow on the heels of maggot damage. Since pupae overwinter in soil, good fall cleanup followed by repeat cultivation of infested soil can greatly reduce root maggot problems the following year.

Where damage occurs every year, rotate crops, cultivate soil well prior to planting, then cover young seedlings with floating row covers as soon as they are set out. Row covers can be left on cabbage-family crops for many weeks until the weather warms. Diatomaceous earth or wood ashes, piled one-quarter inch deep in a broad collar around the base of seedlings, may discourage the adult flies from laying eggs. In large plantings, parasitic nematodes may be effective in halting further damage, but proper timing is critical. The maggots must be actively feeding before parasitic nematodes can be expected to enter their bodies and kill them.

Cabbageworms and Cabbage Loopers

Cabbageworms and cabbage loopers are two similar pests that feed on the leaves of cabbage, broccoli, brussels sprouts, collards, cauliflower, kale, kohlrabi, and occasionally other leafy greens.

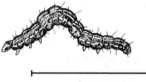

larva: 1¼"/3.2cm

Both are moth larvae. Cabbageworms have tiny feet all along their bodies, while cabbage loopers are inchworms with bodies that loop into an arch as they move along. The adult cabbageworm is a small pale yellow to white moth (also called the cabbage butterfly because it is active during the day); the adult cabbage looper is earthy brown.

Both pests use camouflage as their main means of defense. They are the same color as the light green leaf veins of cabbage-family crops, so you must look carefully to see these nearly invisible pests on the veins when they are not feeding. Their dark green droppings and holes in leaves, especially around leaf margins, tell you that these pests are present.

If you find only a few cabbageworms or cabbage loopers, you may handpick them, a procedure that should be repeated every day in late spring and early fall, when these pests are most active. The worms are much easier to spot on red-leafed varieties, so you might consider red or purple selections of some cabbage-family crops. Also, these pests are easiest to control on plants with smooth leaves. Curled, crinkly leaves give them plenty of places to hide.

Handpicking may not give adequate control, especially when the worms are feeding inside broccoli heads or within the folds of cabbage leaves. When necessary, repeat Bt treatments weekly until the caterpillar populations have been controlled. Floating row covers also provide effective control.

Cankerworms

When you encounter this pest of apple, elm, and other trees, the first clue to its identity is that it is a looper, or inchworm, which arches its body as it moves. In most areas, only two of the many species occur — the spring cankerworm and the fall cankerworm. These two are remarkably similar, but they lay eggs at different times of year. Both weaken trees by feeding on leaves, and both are often kept under control by their many natural enemies, including wasps, flies, and birds.

larva: 1"/2.5cm

If you grow a number of apples or precious ornamental trees, protecting them from cankerworm feeding is relatively easy. The fertile females of both species are wingless and must climb up the trees to lay their eggs on twigs or in bark crevices. The females of the spring cankerworm make this pilgrimage in spring, whereas fall cankerworms do their egg laying in late fall. To catch them, wrap barrier bands (a form of sticky trap) around tree trunks, about three feet above the ground, for the month or so when the females are moving. If you capture many fuzzy half-inch-long grayish adults in these sticky bands, few eggs will be laid.

As a precaution against fall cankerworms, trees also may be sprayed with horticultural oil (the updated form of dormant oil) in late fall and early spring to suffocate the eggs. Should the worms suddenly appear in very large numbers, you can quickly control them with a Bt application. You may wish to tolerate light feeding by cankerworms in large shade trees, as they do little damage and help support many birds and beneficial insects.

Carrot Rust Flies

adult: ¼"/6mm
larva: ⅓"/9mm

This formidable pest came to North America from Europe more than a century ago and has continued to gain strength. The adult is a small, long-legged black fly with a yellow head. This pest usually overwinters as a tiny brown pupal case buried in the soil. In late spring, adults emerge and lay their eggs around the base of carrots, celery, parsnips, and related crops. Those eggs hatch into little maggots that eat the small root hairs and then move on into the main roots. Badly riddled plants wilt because their injured roots cannot keep them adequately supplied with water. If you pull up an infested carrot, the tunnels left by the maggots show a rusty orange color, hence the name of this pest.

Carrot rust flies are most problematic where carrots are grown commercially, for they quickly establish themselves as a resident population, even in cold climates. Rotating crops can help, but because the adults can fly well, they may quickly find your carrots and celery. Keep the area around plants dusted with fresh wood ashes to deter egg laying, and use hot pepper powder as a further deterrent. Spring plantings often take the worst beatings; fall crops may show little damage. Where rust fly problems are chronic and severe, grow carrots and other susceptible crops beneath floating row covers.

Carrot Worms

See **Parsley Worms.**

Caterpillars

There are many different kinds of caterpillars because this is the name applied to the larval stage of many moths and butterflies. They are as numerous and varied as their parents, which flit through the air from earliest spring until winter. Being larvae, caterpillars are almost exclusively leaf-eating machines, with no interest in life beyond food.

Probably because they are so numerous, caterpillars often have many natural enemies. Their most common (and sometimes only) defense against birds and large meat-eating insects is camouflage. Should they venture onto a plant that clashes with their hues, they will be snapped up. Camouflage or not, if they catch the eye of a parasitic wasp or fly ready to lay some eggs, they may find themselves with a terminal backache.

Several caterpillars that often become plant pests are discussed individually in this book, but all caterpillars have two things in common in terms of control. First, although handpicking is tedious, it can accomplish wonders. Frequently, every caterpillar collected is two leaves not eaten. Second, most caterpillars can be eliminated with Bt. When handpicking is just too hard, as when cabbageworms are lodged inside almost-ripe heads of broccoli, Bt can save the day.

Celery Worms

See **Parsley Worms.**

Codling Moths

The codling moth is the mother of the apple worm, a pinkish borer with a brown head that attempts to ruin apples wherever they are grown. It turns up in other fruits, too (pear, quince, crabapple), but it got its name because *codling* is another name for a tiny young apple as it starts to take shape after blossoming. Codling moths are experts at attacking apples when they are exactly at this stage of growth.

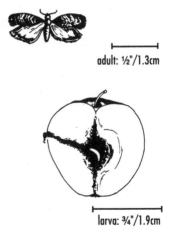

adult: ½"/1.3cm

larva: ¾"/1.9cm

In reality, the moths begin their reproductive quests at about the time apples blossom. Mature pupae emerge as small, variegated, grayish brown moths, exactly the color of apple tree bark. As soon as temperatures become warm enough, they mate and begin laying eggs on the trees, usually on or near the fruits. When the eggs hatch a couple of weeks later, the larvae move to the codlings and usually bore inside, starting at the blossom (bottom) end of the fruit. Many of these fruits subsequently drop, and bits of sawdustlike frass at the bottom end tell you that codling moths are to blame. Later generations may enter apples anywhere on the fruits and remain hidden until the apples are mature.

Only a few codling moths can ruin quite a lot of apples, as each female lays between fifty and two hundred eggs. In mid-spring, when the moths first begin to fly, you may be able to detect their presence using a light trap or a sticky trap. However, phero-mone traps are more effective for detection and quite easy to use.

Beyond trapping, barrier bands may be wrapped around the trunks of apple trees from midsummer onward to trap the mature larvae as they travel down the tree in search of a good place to pupate. When the larvae have eaten their fill, they usually move to bark crevices in the main trunk to pupate.

Because the trunk is such a popular place for codling moths to overwinter, check it thoroughly in late fall and winter. Remove flaking bits of bark to expose the pest. Spraying with dormant oil in late fall and early spring will suffocate some of the pupae.

Many well-known beneficial insects prey on codling moths, including small trichogramma wasps. You can purchase these wasps and release them in large orchards.

Colorado Potato Beetles

Most people are familiar with this black-and-cream-striped beetle, but you may not recognize the ugly orange-red larvae until they are making a mess of homegrown potatoes. An octogenarian neighbor of mine used to call these lar-vae glutton bugs, and the biggest ones certainly resemble well-fattened pigs.

adult: ⅜"/10mm

Resident populations of potato beetles build up over time, so don't be surprised if problems seem to increase year after year. Handpicking can be very effective when you manage to catch a number of adults in mid-spring, when they emerge from hibernating in the soil. The beetles lay orange eggs in groups of over twenty on the undersides or within crevices of potato leaves. Each adult may lay more than five hundred eggs a month. Each one you catch and drop in a can of soapy water means hundreds fewer larvae to deal with later.

The way you grow potatoes can help prevent beetle problems. If at all possible, use a thick mulch of straw. For reasons unknown, populations of beetle larvae on potatoes grown with straw are half those of strawless spuds.

Frequently, you will begin seeing potato beetle adults when your potato plants are about a foot tall. Larvae soon follow; they may be numerous in the new leaves that surround blossoming tips. If you can, handpick these small larvae and squash them or collect them in a can. Do wear a glove when handpicking the largest ones, for they may surprise you by pinching your skin if you attempt to carry them in your hand.

If you have a large planting of infested potatoes, you can use the strain of Bt specially formulated for potato beetle larvae — *Bacillus thuringiensis san diego*. This biological agent kills off young larvae by making them sick when they eat it.

If you are seeing both larvae and large numbers of adult potato beetles, you may use sabadilla dust to bring them under control. Rotenone will work, too, although it presents substantial risks to beneficial insects.

Floating row covers combined with crop rotation will control serious infestations and can help prevent potato beetle problems. You must carefully inspect your plants to make sure no eggs are hiding in the lower leaves before installing the row covers. Even if your inspection reveals no hidden bugs, it's a good idea to check beneath the covers every week or so in late spring to make sure potato beetles are not carrying on their dirty work under cover.

Corn Borers, European

Like several other borers, the European corn borer is the larval form of a moth. It was first imported to the United States in

larva: 1"/2.5cm

1909, and by mid-century it had become a leading pest of corn. The corn borer remains a problem in many areas, although many modern corn varieties contain a chemical that slows the feeding of corn borers and limits their ability to reproduce. Wherever these pale, flesh colored worms with dark dots are frequently seen boring into cornstalks, chewing off tassels, or boring into ears, be sure to choose varieties known to be resistant.

Weather also plays a role, as borers are least problematic following extremely cold winters and cool, wet weather in early summer. The adult moths lay their eggs on corn leaves, and frequent heavy rains knock the eggs off before they can hatch. In a small planting of early sweet corn, forceful spraying with water may suppress this pest.

The adult moths fly at night and may be collected in light traps. The moths are mottled tan and match the hue of corn tassels almost exactly. During the day, a number of natural predators, including tachinid flies and braconid wasps, may attack exposed larvae.

If larvae are exposed and feeding on leaves and tassels, they can often be controlled with timely applications of Bt. Sometimes individual plants become badly infested. When this happens, pull them up and destroy them so that remaining plants will not be bothered by the next generation. Keep weeds out of the corn patch, as weeds will provide preferred areas for egg-laying.

Corn Earworms, Tomato Fruitworms

This pest damages so many commercial crops that it has several names, including cotton bollworm, tobacco budworm, and tomato fruitworm. If none of these host plants is

larva: 1¼"/3.2cm

present, it may even feed on beans. However, its favorite food is corn, particularly the fresh young silks and ear tips of sweet corn.

Good timing is the most important factor to consider when devising a control strategy, especially if you live in the southern half of the country, where earworms are most destructive. The parents of earworms are large, fat-bodied, grayish brown or tan moths. They fly mostly at dusk or on cloudy days. As soon as the first sweet corn silks appear, use a pheromone trap or light trap to detect their presence. These moths lay hundreds of eggs on corn silks, although only a few survive to cause damage. Actual counts of adult moths caught in traps may be quite low.

The next step is to kill the larvae before they enter young ears. About a week after sweet corn silks appear (if the weather is warm), eggs laid by adults hatch and begin to feed. This is the time to fill a spray bottle with Bt and thoroughly douse each silk. Repeat the application one week later. Another control technique is dropping about ¼ teaspoon of mineral oil on the corn silks of each ear after the silks have wilted but before they begin to dry.

Growing varieties that form a tight husk that extends over the tip of the ear can further deter feeding, as the earworms are denied the room they need to grow. If your corn does become infested, usually there is but one worm per ear, as these larvae are cannibalistic. Shuck and pop off the tips of infested ears right after harvesting, and you will enjoy plenty of high-quality homegrown sweet corn.

Several companion crops have strong reputations for repelling corn earworms. These include pumpkins, marigolds, and dill. Flowers that attract caterpillar enemies such as small wasps and flies can be of value in preventing earworm problems.

Cucumber Beetles

Several species of cucumber beetles wreak havoc in gardens. The most common ones are small yellow-and-black-striped cucumber beetles, often seen ranging about the garden until they find

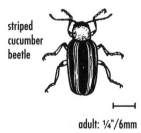

striped cucumber beetle

adult: ¼"/6mm

squash or cucumber plants. When adults find host plants, they feed on the leaves and flowers and lay eggs in the soil beneath the plants. Within two weeks, those eggs hatch, and the larvae begin feeding on cucurbit roots.

Spotted cucumber beetles are larger, and they also feed on squash and cucumber flowers and vines, but the preferred host plant for spotted cucumber beetle larvae is corn. In larval form, this pest (along with several other species of cucumber beetles) is better known as the corn rootworm.

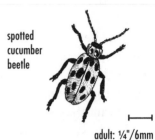

spotted cucumber beetle

adult: ¼"/6mm

The worst thing about both striped and spotted cucumber beetles is their ability to spread disease. Striped cucumber beetles are prime carriers of bacterial wilt, a common and incurable disease of cucumbers. Both cucumber beetles can spread cucumber mosaic virus as they fly from one plant to another.

With cucumbers, you can limit beetle problems by planting varieties described as nonbitter. The bitter compounds present in most cucurbits act as a feeding stimulant for cucumber beetles. If the bitter compounds are not present, the beetles are less enthusiastic feeders.

An equally good strategy is to cover susceptible plants with floating row covers until they start flowering. Interplant radishes among cucumbers so that they, too, will begin flowering at about the time the row covers will be removed. I can't explain it, but radishes seem to repel cucumber beetles and many other pests. In some areas, cucumber beetles are attracted to calendulas. Start a few of these cold-tolerant flowers early so that they begin blooming just as cucumber beetles emerge. Use a butterfly net to capture the beetles from your calendula trap crop, as they are very difficult to catch by hand.

If all else fails, you can poison heavy infestations with sabadilla or rotenone. For best results, treat the plants in the morning, just before the beetles become most active. At midday, cover the plants with floating row covers or sheets to keep the beetles within the treated area and to keep helpful insects from visiting the contaminated blossoms. Remove the covers after three days, when it should be safe for pollinators to resume their good deeds.

Cutworms

After you have spent weeks growing tomato or cabbage plants from seed, it is quite distressing to find the plants felled

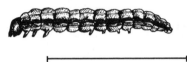

larva: 1½" – 2"/3.8cm – 5.1cm

like little trees within days after you set them out. Some corpses may be present but sadly shriveled, while others will have disappeared altogether. This is the work of cutworms — various moth larvae that are among the most inefficient eaters in the insect world. A few bites and they are done, which means a single cutworm may kill a dozen plants in a few days' time.

Fortunately, this damage is easily prevented. When you transplant seedlings, encircle each one with a protective collar made from a paper cup with the bottom punched out. Another method is to stick a toothpick or twig down the side of the plant stem. When the cutworm attempts to encircle the stem to girdle it, the tough wood gets in the way.

When beans and other seed-sown crops are bothered by cutworms, investigate the soil right around the casualties at the earliest possible time. Use a kitchen fork to stir the soil within six inches of the felled seedlings, and you may find the culprit before it can do further damage. Grow some extra seedlings to replace those toppled by cutworms.

You also can try going on a night hunt for cutworms. Late in the evening, take a flashlight and bug-gathering can and pick off any caterpillars you find in and around seedlings. Cutworms come in many shades, and some climb up plants at night to eat the leaves. Handpick these, too. All cutworms are soft-bodied, hairless caterpillars.

Usually cutworms are most numerous in soil that has recently been covered with grass. For a long-term management strategy,

keep your garden free of weeds in late summer and fall, and cultivate twice in spring before planting. Using a mulch of oak leaves
or other acidic material also can discourage this pest. And, as
always, encourage natural predators of cutworms, which include
braconid wasps, tachinid flies, and ground beetles.

Dragonflies

adult: size varies

Large, fast-flying dragonflies,
in iridescent shades of black, blue,
and green, are regular visitors to
many gardens, although their primary hunting grounds (and larval
habitats) are streams, lakes, and
rivers. They are harmless unless you happen to be a mosquito, fly,
or little moth. More than one hundred mosquitoes have been
counted in the stomachs of large dragonflies. Dragonfly nymphs
have been observed eating sixty mosquito larvae in ten minutes.
The presence of dragonflies in the garden is clearly a positive sign,
especially in the heat of summer, when mosquitoes sometimes
become the rulers of the garden's airspace.

Earthworms

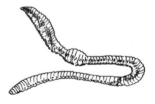

adult: size varies

The earthworm is not an insect
but belongs to its own phylum, called
Annelida, which includes more than
six thousand species of segmented
worms. Earthworms have evolved over
millions of years, and it's hard to imagine that any species you
could import would be superior to the strains that already exist in
your soil. Rather than rearing hybrids or strains from far away,
gardeners should cultivate a spirit of stewardship toward their own
homegrown earthworms.

Many books of the nineteenth century recommended destroying earthworms because they were believed to be injurious to
plants. They do ingest much plant material, but most of it is dead.
Thanks to Charles Darwin's research, we now know how valuable

the earthworm is and understand its unique contribution to the health of plants.

Earthworms enrich the soil both chemically and physically. As earthworms eat, they convert dead and decaying material into castings that are rich in minerals, available in a form that plants can use immediately. They also travel up and down through the soil, often coming to the surface to feed at night and then tunneling back down in the daytime, when their primary enemies — birds — are on the prowl. Very wet weather drives them toward the surface, for earthworms are at constant risk of drowning. All this movement results in numerous open passageways within the soil, through which air and rain can easily pass, thus improving drainage.

Many books recommend that gardeners rear earthworms in specially made boxes. Indoor boxes allow cold-climate gardeners to continue composting through the winter, but by counting worms in various habitats, I have learned that there are easier ways. Perhaps the best approach is to pile stable manure atop the soil in winter. In my experience, the biggest, fattest earthworms are found not in a compost heap or worm bed, but in the foot of soil directly beneath manure piles. When the rotted manure is moved, those worms disperse through the garden to carry on their good works. If manure is not handy, weathered leaves mixed with a little soil are almost as attractive.

Earthworm counts also are quite high beneath grass. Grass has so many little roots that it provides a banquet for earthworms. To keep them happy in your garden, plant grassy cover crops such as annual rye or wheat when you do not need the space for other plants.

The only place you do not want to see earthworms is in containers filled with plants that like to be somewhat root-bound, such as ferns and summer flowers. The only food that exists for them in this environment is the roots of your plants. If the container is large and the root space is roomy, there is no problem. But when roots are crowded, it's a good idea to tamp out the plant, keeping the root ball intact, pick out the worms, and return them to open soil.

Earwigs

The earwig is easy to recognize by the pair of pincers it carries on its rear. Earwigs do double duty as beneficial and harmful insects. They are important aphid predators on fruit trees. They consume small insect larvae, but they also chew on young vegetable seedlings and many flowers, including dahlias and hollyhocks. Occasionally, they move indoors and become a nuisance in the pantry.

adult: ½"/1.3cm

Outdoors, earwigs are nocturnal, and their habit of hiding in dark places during the day makes them easy to trap. They like to climb upward to a place that is high, dry, and dark. Hollow bamboo stems hung about the garden can attract them, as can rolled newspapers. You can make another trap with a bit of dry moss in a flowerpot, inverted and stuck on a stake in the garden. Or try hanging partially opened matchboxes on stakes. In the morning, empty any trapped earwigs (from any of the above traps) into a pail of hot soapy water. Be sure to release any beneficial ground beetles unharmed.

To rid plants of earwigs, a spray made of garlic and soap, applied at sundown, can be highly effective. If earwigs become a problem in kitchen cabinets, try setting out boric acid to poison them. See Chapter 5 for garlic brew and boric acid recipes.

Fall Webworms

larva: 1"/2.5cm

The nests of fall webworms are ugly, which is probably the main reason to remove them from trees in your yard. The nests may appear in virtually any fruit or shade tree that is not an evergreen and tend to be numerous in pecans and hickories.

Unlike tent caterpillars, which leave their nests to feed on tree leaves, fall webworms eat only the leaves within their nests. The nests soon become dotted with worm droppings, which make them an eyesore. However, from a plant's point of view, this pest is not so bad. The first generation, which lives during the summer months, is usually quite small. The larger fall generation eats leaves that will be dropped by the trees within a few weeks anyway.

If you wish, you can gather up the nests with a wooden pole with nails driven in the end. Swirl this device in the nest, then scrape off the tent with sticks. Place it in a bucket of very hot water to kill the worms.

If you use barrier bands (sticky bands) to capture adult canker-worms, you also may see fall webworms in your traps, as the fully grown worms crawl down the trees when they are ready to pupate in late fall. The adult form of this pest is a moth that emerges in spring after spending the winter in a silken cocoon.

Fireflies

The fireflies, or lightning bugs, that flash and sparkle on summer evenings are neither flies nor bugs, but rather very primitive beetles. The species we call fireflies use their little light boxes to attract mates. Depending on the species, the actual color of the lights may be yellow, orange, or yellowish green.

Adult fireflies pose no threat to plants, though they may be seen feeding on flower nectar or pollen. The larvae of many fireflies are important pest predators; they consume eggs of slugs and grasshoppers, as well as small maggots and caterpillars.

A very similar insect called the soldier beetle is a more aggressive predator. The soldier beetle looks very much like a firefly, but does not have a light organ. Some soldier beetles do feed lightly on plants, but as larvae they are mostly interested in the same insect eggs and soft-bodied larvae relished by fireflies. Firefly populations often decline after midsummer; soldier beetles are most numerous in late summer, when they may often be seen on goldenrod and milkweed blossoms.

Flea Beetles

As soon as radish or turnip leaves appear in spring, the flea beetle hops on and begins to make tiny holes in them. There are a dozen common species of flea beetles,

H

adult: 1/16" – 1/8"/1.6mm – 3.2mm

including some that attack only certain crops, such as spinach, potatoes, or eggplant. Some are general feeders, as happy putting holes in tomato leaves as in corn. Flea beetles are usually most numerous in spring, and populations decline as summer progresses.

Despite their small size, flea beetles are very mobile, thanks to strong rear legs that enable them to hop away energetically at the slightest disturbance. They often move throughout the garden, tasting various plants until they find a favorite.

For the most part, the damage done by flea beetles is cosmetic, and most plants quickly recover. The biggest health risk flea beetles pose to plants comes from their ability to spread diseases, but this is generally not a problem in home gardens. If you feel compelled to do something about flea beetles, try covering a small board or sheet of cardboard with a sticky substance such as Tangle-Trap or even honey and holding it above infested plants as you gently jiggle them to get the flea beetles hopping. For particularly susceptible plants, such as eggplant seedlings, use cloches (glass or plastic covers) or floating row covers to protect plants for three weeks or so after you set them out in late spring.

Four-Lined Plant Bugs

This insect is closely related to the tarnished plant bug (page 94). Its appearance differs in that the four-lined plant bug has four longitudinal black lines, alternating with bright yellow ones, down its back. In my garden, the four-lined plant bug makes rows of little brown spots on leaves of all composite flowers in spring — even daisies and coreopsis. Later in summer, I've seen a number of them apparently living in a bed of plume celosia. I saw no evidence that they were doing serious harm to the celosia, so I left them alone.

adult: ⅜"/10mm

Admittedly, little spots on the leaves of flowers aren't pretty, and it's possible that the four-lined plant bug could get out of hand. If that happens, it would be prudent to capture some in a butterfly net and dispose of them, or dust them once with sabadilla.

Fruit Flies

adult: to ¼"/6mm

Several small flies lay eggs in immature fruits, which hatch into little fruit-eating maggots. Apples, cherries, and blueberries are the targets of specific species of fruit flies, though the same fly that lays her eggs in apples may sometimes bother peaches, nectarines, plums, and pears.

The fruit flies whose young are known as fruit maggots are slightly smaller than a housefly, dark brown in color, and have light and dark markings on their wings. They overwinter as pupae in soil and emerge in summer. After mating, adults lay eggs in immature fruits, and the maggots hatch and feed inside. Some of these fruits drop, but others may mature and have dark tunnels inside them.

Many natural predators, including braconid and ichneumon wasps, prey on fruit flies. With apples, the flies are often more successful invading relatively soft-fleshed early varieties than hard winter apples.

Traps known as red spheres, which are basically sticky traps made to look like apples, are an easy way to trap adult flies before they lay eggs in fruits. Hang these traps in trees in early summer, soon after the green fruits have begun to grow. For fruit flies on cherries and blueberries, the best strategy is to pick and destroy infested fruits as soon as you see them, and to encourage natural predators by growing plenty of pollen-rich flowers in and near the orchard.

A much smaller fruit fly, which has no stripes on its wings, can become irritating indoors when you bring fruit inside to ripen. This species especially likes pears, as well as any other fruits that become so ripe that they are on the verge of fermentation.

Should you have a large collection of peaches or pears to ripen at room temperature, cover them with a piece of floating row cover, tucked under at the edges. If flies congregate on the fabric, gather them with the vacuum cleaner. Every day or so, lift the row cover and vacuum up any flies hiding underneath. The little flies are so fragile that the turbulence of the vacuum kills them.

Grasshoppers

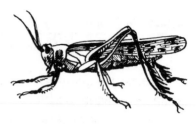

adult: size varies

No one who has lived through a scourge of grasshoppers can ever forget the long, hot summer days when every vestige of green gradually disappeared — first from the herb garden, then the vegetable garden and orchard, and finally the cornfields. Even in small yards, it doesn't take many grasshoppers to do a lot of damage.

With grasshoppers, this often happens for two or three consecutive summers. Populations often build up quickly, resulting in unexpected swarms that can break any gardener's heart.

How do they do it? Grasshoppers mate in late summer, and the females lay big clusters of eggs in the soil. These eggs hatch in spring, and the little grasshoppers eat for six to eight weeks, then molt several times. This is when they really become noticeable and start tasting, then devouring, every leaf they find to their liking.

Numerous homemade repellents have been tried against grasshoppers, with very limited success. Grasshoppers like plants that most other insects find noxious, even marigolds and wormwood. A partial list of failed homemade preparations includes soapsuds, rue or wormwood tea, urine, lime plus wood ashes, castor oil, and tar.

One natural insecticide can be helpful if you want to protect a few plants from grasshoppers. Sabadilla dust often will kill grasshoppers, especially the young ones.

A better idea is to enlist the help of some chickens or ducks in collecting grasshoppers. This, too, works best in early summer when grasshoppers are small.

Another idea is to use lightweight floating row covers to protect plants from grasshoppers. I often must do this in late summer, when I'm trying to get fall vegetables and flowers up and growing. Since grasshoppers hop (as opposed to crawling), the edges of the covers do not have to be buried. I usually place a row cover loosely over a bed and weight down the corners with clay flowerpots.

In a bad grasshopper year, you might make mental notes of plants that are not bothered by grasshoppers. Last summer, they stripped everything in one of my flower beds but the nicotiana. I even saw one eating a jalapeño pepper. Watch closely, and you may discover some highly resistant plants among your personal favorites.

Some natural control methods work poorly because grasshoppers are so mobile, often jumping twelve feet in a single bound. However, if your property is large and your grasshopper population is huge, you might try a protozoan (single-celled animal) called *Nosema locustae*. These living organisms are "fed" to young grasshoppers in spring. For the best results, the contaminated bait material must be put out just after the grasshoppers begin to feed. A full month may pass before the grasshoppers start dying. Grasshoppers that survive may pass on the illness to their eggs. Where grasshoppers are a chronic problem, year after year, put out fresh batches of *Nosema* each spring.

In small yards where grasshoppers may easily move in from other people's property, the best yearlong control strategy is to handpick your grasshoppers. Especially go after the biggest ones you can find in August, for these are most likely the females who will soon be laying eggs. Throw your captives in a cricket cage, then take them on a little fishing trip.

Ground Beetles

One of the most attractive families in the insect world is the group called ground beetles (Carabidae). These long-legged, hard-shelled beetles are often seen loping along the ground as though on urgent errands. In reality, they are probably simply running for shelter, as they prefer to conduct all their activities under cover of night. Ground beetles are overwhelmingly beneficial because most

adult: 1"/2.5cm

species are indiscriminate eaters of caterpillars and other soft-bodied larvae. However, a few do eat seeds and berries. More than twelve hundred species occur in North America. The *Calosoma* beetle was imported to control gypsy moths in New England.

If you lay boards atop the soil to trap slugs, you may be fostering ground beetles in the process, for they like the daytime shelter beneath boards, stones, and logs. Timbers around raised beds are popular summer homes. Some ground beetles live to be two to three years old.

Ground beetles are easily identified, but you should know the larvae, too. They also eat caterpillars. Larvae usually are an inch long and clearly segmented, with legs clustered toward the front of their bodies. The head is quite distinct from the rest of the body, with dangerous-looking mouthparts. They are really quite ugly, especially when compared to the shiny iridescent creatures they are destined to become.

Grubs

Hundreds of species of beetles spend one, two, or even three years of their lives as fat, usually curled, white soil-dwelling grubs. Some feed on dead vegetation; others eat living roots of grasses, weeds, and other plants. Some of the most common grubs are larvae of June beetles, Japanese beetles, or Asiatic gar-

June beetle larva:
size varies

den beetles, but grubs of different species look so much alike that trying to identify them is an exercise in frustration.

In general, the presence of a few grubs is acceptable, for they fill an important niche in the network of subterranean life. Yet too many grubs can spell disaster for a lawn, cornfield, or bed of strawberries.

Because grubs are partial to grass roots, they are most numerous below meadows and lawns. When a grassy area is to be transformed into garden space, be sure to cultivate it very well the previous fall. Cultivation by itself will kill some grubs, then birds will join you in your quest to de-grub your new garden space.

When you dig any soil in preparation for planting in spring, pick out the grubs you turn up. Simply toss them into a container — box, jar, or bucket — and let them sit in the sun until dead. I often find rather large grubs at the bottom of my compost heap. Even though I'm certain they are only eating dead plant material, I pick them out anyway. Incidentally, once you convince children that grubs are harmless to people, they make fine grub gatherers.

Milky spore disease is an effective control for large infestations of Japanese beetle or June beetle grubs. See the entries for the **Asiatic garden beetle** (page 39), **June beetle** (page 69), and **Japanese beetle** (page 67) for details on these individual species.

Gypsy Moths

adult: 1¾"/4.5cm
larva: to 2"/5.1cm

The gypsy moth is mostly an enemy of forest trees, but it occasionally chooses a beloved yard tree as its victim. Gypsy moth larvae — dark caterpillars with hair in tufts — eat hundreds of species of trees and shrubs, including evergreens. At their worst, they can kill a tree by stripping off all its leaves. Conifers have an especially hard time recovering.

Should gypsy moths show up in your yard in large numbers, there are several things you can do. Eggs hatch and larvae begin to feed in early summer. If you catch the infestation early enough, you can spray the caterpillars with Bt.

Frequently, the caterpillars climb down the tree after a night's feeding and spend the day hiding in the grass. Barrier bands (burlap) or sticky traps, attached firmly to tree trunks, can capture some of these travelers. You also may capture some adult females this way, as they are so fat-bodied that they usually crawl from place to place instead of flying.

At the end of a bad gypsy moth summer, inspect all trees closely for the presence of egg masses, which look like inch-long bits of beige suede attached to tree bark. Scrape them off and destroy them. Each egg mass you destroy represents four hundred or more unborn larvae.

Harlequin Bugs

These colorful bugs resemble their other stink bug cousins, but have bold orange-and-black markings on their backs. They puncture leaves and stems to suck plant juices and may leave small, ragged holes in cabbage-family crops as well as squash, tomatoes, and beans. They are only found in warmer states.

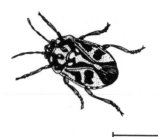

adult: ½"/1.3cm

Damage is worst on broccoli and cabbage that remain in the garden until early summer, when these bugs are most active. In many areas, you can escape this pest entirely by planting fast-maturing varieties early. However, harlequin bugs may again become a problem in the fall, when they discover your young turnips and cabbage set out in late summer.

For fall control, you can try sowing a small trap crop of turnips or cabbage a couple of weeks before you would normally plant them. Should harlequin bugs congregate there, throw a blanket or sheet of floating row cover over the plants to trap the bugs, then gather them up in the cool of the morning.

Sabadilla dust can control harlequin bugs and other shield bugs, but it should be used only when needed, to avoid harming native populations of beneficial insects. A few harlequin bugs feeding on random garden plants will not do much damage and can usually be left alone.

Honeybees

Of all the living creatures that share your garden space, none is more preoccupied with the welfare of your plants than the hardworking honeybee. Its sole mission in the garden is to gather nectar and pollen, and in passing from flower to flower, the

adult: ¾"/1.9cm

honeybee spreads bits of pollen just where it is needed most. Honeybees do come equipped with stingers, but they seldom use them unless their lives, or their hives, are threatened. When a honeybee stings, its life is over, as the use of the stinger tears up the equivalent of its spinal cord.

All gardeners must learn to differentiate between honeybees and wasps, the latter being more dangerous (yet also beneficial). Honeybees are fatter and hairier than yellow jacket wasps and have a more faded yellowish coloring. In summer, honeybees often have packets of yellow pollen attached to their rear legs, whereas wasps do not. See the entry on wasps (page 98) for more insights on how these creatures live.

Honeybees usually manage to find gardens, but if you doubt your resident population is sufficient, be sure to plant plenty of flowers, corn, and other crops that attract them. If you are allergic to bee stings, avoid working in the garden in midmorning, when bees are busiest.

Hornworms, Tomato Hornworms

Practically everyone who has ever raised a garden has shuddered with horror at the sight of the tomato hornworm because of its size and voraciousness. A single hornworm can consume several tomato leaves in one day, and a small crew of them has no trouble completely defoliating a plant in a week's time.

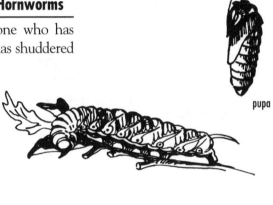

pupa

larva: 3" – 4"/7.6cm – 10.2cm

If not for our love of tomatoes, we would certainly admire this pest's good looks. Two species are commonly seen on garden tomatoes — one with eight stripes and a black horn, and one with seven stripes and a red horn. Although some people are intimidated by these horns, don't be afraid. Hornworms can't bite or sting people, although they will try to frighten you by wagging their fierce-looking horns.

Tomato hornworms are the larvae of a very large moth that is about the size of a hummingbird. In late spring, the moth lays individual green eggs on the undersides of tomato leaves. These eggs are so few and scattered that they are almost impossible to find. The worms, too, remain hidden when they are very small. However, as they gain weight (from eating so many tomato leaves), they become more noticeable. When you see their dark green droppings littering leaves and the ground beneath your tomato plants, it's time to embark on a hornworm hunt.

Once you find them, hornworms are easy to handpick and drown or squash to death with your foot. Bt will kill them if they are small, but once they are more than two inches long, you should rely on your handpicking talents to control them.

If you are lucky, some of the hornworms you find will have little white cocoons attached to their backs. These are pupating braconid wasps, a highly desirable predatory insect. Instead of destroying parasitized hornworms and their valuable baggage, keep them in jars. As you pinch and prune tomato plants, place fresh leaves in the jars to sustain the worms. You also might move parasitized hornworms onto a tomato plant you are willing to sacrifice. By midsummer, I usually have a number of volunteer tomato plants of unknown lineage, and I use a couple of these as braconid nurseries.

In years when hornworm problems are especially severe, be sure to cultivate the tomato patch well at the end of the season. Hornworms overwinter as dark brown pupae, one to two inches long. In late fall, turn the soil several times to expose the pupae to weather and birds.

Hover Flies

See **Syrphid Flies.**

Ichneumon Wasps

Though often referred to as flies, the ichneumons are true wasps. Some species are too small to see well, but others are more than an inch long. Most are black with red or yellow spots and bands. Their appearance is quite sinister, as the dis-

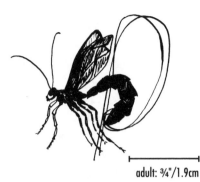

adult: ¾"/1.9cm

tinguishing characteristic of ichneumons is a very long ovipositor (we tend to mistake this for a stinger). Rather than waste the ovipositor on stinging people, the ichneumon uses it to deposit eggs inside borers and other prey that may be hidden inside plants, accessing them via the victim's own entry hole. In some species, the ovipositor is so long that the wasp must carry it curled up around the rear portion of its body.

Ichneumon adults feed lightly and harmlessly on flower nectar, and planting plenty of flowers is the best way to lure them to your garden. In a garden filled with diverse plants and insects, a few ichneumons will certainly be present. Most of their good deeds go unseen, for the eggs and larvae usually develop entirely inside host insects — caterpillars, borers, aphids, maggots, and beetle larvae. As the baby ichneumons feed, they weaken their hosts but do not kill them until the ichneumons are almost mature themselves. Miraculously, ichneumon larvae feed inside the host while avoiding its essential organs, thus ensuring their own survival. Of course, this means that they do not kill pests instantly, but they make certain that the parasitized host does not survive and reproduce.

Japanese Beetles

Japanese beetles are a devastating pest in the mid-Atlantic area and can show up in alarming numbers anywhere in the eastern half of the

adult: ½"/1.3cm

larva: ¾"/1.9cm

United States. Where they are established, they emerge without fail in midsummer and proceed to devour roses, peaches, and 250 other garden plants. During their peak period, which lasts a month or more, dozens of beetles may be seen eating a plant on any sunny day.

Japanese beetles are smaller than other garden beetles and usually have shiny greenish heads and backs covered by copper-brown wings. The larvae are small white grubs that eat grass roots during the spring months.

Because the larvae are so fond of grass, the beetles usually lay their eggs in turf or pastures in late summer. The hatchlings usually thrive in new lawns, where the naturally occurring parasitic bacterium called milky spore has yet to become established. Should you be gardening near a new lawn or any large, grassy spot, the first thing to do is to inoculate the soil with milky spore, which is packaged as a powder that should be scattered over grass just before a rain. Over time, milky spore disease will cause a serious population decline among Japanese beetle larvae. It is harmless to earthworms.

Pheromone traps are very popular for trapping adult beetles, but there is some controversy over whether they make beetle problems better or worse. Should you decide to try traps, be sure to locate them at least thirty feet away from crop plants. The traps always attract plenty of beetles, but some gardeners feel they may attract beetles that would not stop by if the traps were not present.

Where Japanese beetles are an occasional problem on specific plants, floating row covers can keep them at bay. Or try laying sheets beneath plants on a cool morning, then shaking the plants until the beetles fall to the ground. Gather them up in the sheets and dump them in a pail of steaming hot soapy water.

If shaking is impractical, you can often kill many Japanese beetles by dusting them with sabadilla or rotenone. If you opt for the chemical solution, be forewarned that it will control your problem for only a day or two. After that, you'll either have to re-treat the plants or seek some other solution. The usual method of covering treated plants with floating row covers is difficult to use with roses (a favorite of Japanese beetles) because the prickly plants easily tear holes in the fragile row covers.

The only good thing about Japanese beetles is that their feeding period is short. By late summer, the adults die and the new generation of grubs have gone below ground, where they stay for ten months in most areas.

June Beetles

adult: ¾"/1.9cm

You may call them June beetles, May beetles, or June bugs. These are the common brown beetles that gather near your porch light on summer nights, possibly inadvertently alighting on your head. In their larval stage, they are among the most common soil-dwelling white grubs.

Adults that are not hanging around your porch lights may spend their evenings eating leaves and flowers in your garden. Usually they choose roses and their relatives, including bramble fruits and strawberries. The grubs prefer a diet of grass roots. Since corn is a grass, it is sometimes injured when large numbers of grubs find and devour its tender roots. To diagnose this problem, simply pull or dig up a corn plant that is not growing well and inspect it. If many grubs are present, you may have found the problem.

Should you choose to eliminate some adults, a light trap will work very well. Or handpick the beetles at night, using a flashlight. (They spend their days hiding in the soil and among weeds.) Long-term reduction in the numbers of June beetles living both above and below ground often can be achieved by inoculating the soil with milky spore disease, which also kills larvae of the Japanese beetle, a much more formidable pest.

Lacewings

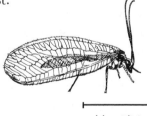

adult: ¾"/1.9cm

Lacewing larvae so efficiently clean up aphid infestations that they are commonly known as aphid lions. The larvae are rather ferocious-looking yellow-brown creatures with tufts of stiff hair sticking out in all directions, and they feed exclusively on protein-rich insects. The delicate adults are light consumers of flower nectar and pollen and honeydew from aphids. They may be green or brown in color, resembling small dragonflies.

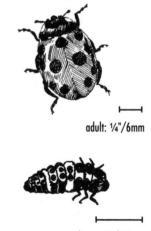

larva: ½"/1.3cm

eggs on leaf

Lacewing eggs are easily identified, as no other insect places its eggs on stiff threads that stand out from plant leaves. The larvae also may be seen from late spring onward, wherever aphids congregate.

To encourage lacewings, grow plenty of nectar-rich flowers and other plants that produce a lot of pollen. Purchased lacewing eggs are sold commercially, but wait until several weeks after your last frost before distributing them among plants that are infested with aphids. The best use for purchased lacewing eggs is probably an enclosed greenhouse, where they help control not only aphids but also mealybugs, scale, and assorted mites. Wild or introduced lacewings do the same good deeds in an open garden.

Lady Beetles, Ladybugs

The jewel-like scarlet beetles that show up in bright contrast to the green leaves of the garden are among the most gifted aphid hunters in the animal kingdom. Overwintered adults emerge starting in mid-spring, after aphid colonies have become established on many plants (aphids are usually the first pests of the season to appear in noticeable numbers). The lady beetles seek them out and lay eggs quite near the aphids. Those eggs hatch within a week, and the lady beetle larvae start devouring aphids.

adult: ¼"/6mm

larva: ½"/1.3cm

Most gardeners recognize the most common type of lady beetle, which has a red-orange back and black head. Yet the larvae are much more uncomely in appearance, usually black and orange, less than one-half inch long, and resembling the related Mexican bean beetle larva in configuration.

Some species of lady beetles specialize in controlling pests other than aphids. Offbeat species may appear where scale or mealybugs are abundant. The more common lady beetles will change their dietary preferences, at least for a time, in response to an unusual but copious food supply.

You can import lady beetles to your garden, where they will probably provide good short-term control of aphids. However, once the food supply runs short, they may leave for better hunting grounds. I think the best approach to fostering this fine friend is to make sure your garden is an attractive place for them. When you notice that they like a particular plant, include it where you can. In my garden, lady beetles are clearly attracted to sweet corn and leafy greens. As long as I plant these two crops, lady beetles are always in good supply, and I have never considered buying more of them.

Leafhoppers

adult: ¼"/6mm

These tiny insects come in many forms, but the ones that give gardeners the most trouble are either potato leafhoppers on potatoes and beans or beet leafhoppers, which spread viral diseases such as curly top virus. Both are very small, greenish wedge-shaped insects that hop about wildly when disturbed.

Potato leafhoppers cause a condition called hopperburn, in which leaf tips, and then leaf margins, turn brown and die. This occurs when leafhopper nymphs and adults feed. Working exclusively on leaf undersides, thousands of leafhoppers destroy leaf veins and use the dead, curled-down edges for shelter. To identify the pest, wave a piece of cardboard covered with Tangle-Trap (see **Sticky Traps,** page 127) or honey over the damaged plants, stirring the foliage as you go. Then use a magnifying glass to identify the leafhoppers you catch.

If hopperburn is in progress, stop the damage with soap. First rinse the plants well with a strong spray of water aimed at leaf undersides, then apply an insecticidal soap. Homemade herbal or garlic spray with soap added also can work well. Repeat after three days.

Beet leafhoppers do not appear in great numbers, but they do carry the curly top virus around the gardens of the West. When new growth of tomatoes, beans, or melons develops brown spots, shrivels, and dies, curly top has struck. Once infected, plants cannot recover. Pull up sick plants right away and destroy them.

If you live where this pest is problematic, grow tomatoes under floating row covers when they are young. Later, when the weather becomes very hot and leafhoppers appear, keep plants partially shaded. Leafhoppers love full sun.

Because all types of leafhoppers move so quickly and are so small, controlling them with insecticides is seldom worth the trouble. You might get rid of a few, but not without incurring unwanted casualties among your resident beneficials. More leafhoppers will likely appear, requiring several repetitions of an unwinnable battle.

Insects known as treehoppers have a basic build similar to that of leafhoppers, but they carry odd-shaped humps on their backs. These entertaining little creatures lay eggs in small twigs and feed on tree leaves, but the damage they cause is slight. It is fascinating, however, to study the crazy shapes and patterns of their backpacks, which scientists refer to as pronotums.

Leaf Miners

Pale tracings on leaves that look like the meandering trail of a worm are the work of leaf miners — actually

leaf miner trails in leaf   adult: ⅛"/3.2mm

tiny fly larvae that are difficult to catch in the act of eating. They lurk inside the leaf, often as whitish bulges, and are most often seen on birch trees, beets, columbine, Swiss chard, and spinach. The adults are small flies that emerge in early summer.

Leaf miner damage is not pretty but is rarely so serious that it significantly undermines plant health. Should you discover the miners while they are actively feeding, pinch off infested leaves and burn them. Otherwise, it is probably prudent to leave the plants alone, as even mined leaves continue to function on the plant's behalf. Should miners attack a certain crop every summer without fail, keep track of when the damage starts and cover the plants with floating row covers during the weeks when miners are expected to appear. Following an outbreak of miners on spinach or beets, harvest the crop at the earliest possible time and cultivate the soil very well. Once miners have eaten their fill, they drop to the soil to pupate. When these pupae are disturbed and exposed, many natural predators, including birds, will likely take care of this pest.

Leaf Rollers

Any little caterpillar that rolls leaves into little cigar shapes, binds them with webbing, and takes up residence inside can be called a leaf roller. Few beneficials of vegetable and flower gardens handle themselves this way, so don't hesitate to pluck off such leaves and destroy them.

Grapes, apples, and other fruits have their own special leaf-roller enemies that become so numerous that they damage more than their share of leaves. Fruit-tree leaf rollers overwinter as eggs attached to stems and twigs. Two applications of dormant oil, one in late fall and the other in late winter, will control them. The red-banded leaf roller overwinters on the ground, beneath leaves and in mulch, so the best way to control this species is to clean the area beneath fruit trees in late fall and replace old mulches with fresh material.

Should either species appear in abundance on fruit-tree leaves, immediately treat them with Bt. If you wait too long, protective webbing around their little nests will provide so much shelter that many of the worms may survive this treatment unharmed. Parents of both species are furry little moths, which are so fast moving that they are impossible to pursue.

Mealybugs

For most plant lovers, the first encounter with mealybugs occurs on houseplants, especially tropicals such as scheffleras. The cottony-white scalelike insects hug the stems, sucking plant juices. To get rid of them, dip a cotton swab in alcohol and

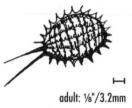

adult: ⅛"/3.2mm

touch it to each bug. The alcohol penetrates the waxy coating and kills the bugs within days. Small ones that you did not see the first time may appear after a few weeks, indicating the need for a second treatment.

Other types of mealybugs may appear on grapes, citrus trees, and other fruits. If you act promptly when the bugs first appear, a strong spray of water followed by the use of an insecticidal soap will radically reduce their number. After that, natural predators will likely keep the mealybugs in check. There is no single time of year to expect citrus mealybugs. Because citrus fruits are grown in mild winter climates, the bugs are able to proliferate all year long.

With grapes, do all you can to keep the vines clean. In small plantings, handpicking and spot spraying with insecticidal soap is usually sufficient. In climates where winters are cold, mealybugs are seldom a problem on outdoor plants.

Mexican Bean Beetles

Sooner or later, almost every gardener in North America is likely to see Mexican bean beetles on his or her bush, pole, or lima beans. The mustard-

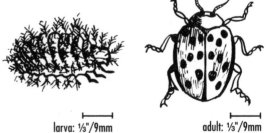

larva: ⅓"/9mm   adult: ⅓"/9mm

yellow adults with black spots often pass unnoticed in early summer, when they emerge from overwintering in plant debris. But the females quickly find beans on which to feed and lay their eggs. Masses of yellow eggs appear on leaf undersides, usually between leaf veins, in groups of forty or more. In unlucky years, problems become epidemic, as each female may lay five hundred or more eggs before she is exhausted.

Gardeners usually don't know there is trouble until two weeks after the eggs are laid, when the larvae hatch and spread out to feed. The spiny, bloblike yellow larvae rasp away at the undersides of bean leaves until only see-through skeletonized tissue remains. Meanwhile, wandering adults are still laying eggs. Left uncontrolled, Mexican bean beetles will weaken plants so severely that they will stop producing before their time.

The more adults you can catch in spring, the fewer larvae you will have to deal with in summer. Get to know these beetles — larvae and adults look a lot like their lady beetle cousin, only bigger and yellowish. Mexican bean beetles are a challenge to catch because they can fly. Morning is a good time to catch and crush them.

If larvae are busily feeding, you have a choice of several methods. Handpicking is one option. While you're at it, destroy any egg masses you find by rubbing them gently with your fingers. Elderly leaves that are hopelessly infested may be picked off and destroyed.

Herbal sprays probably won't help repel feeding larvae because the little critters get constant messages from their digestive tracts telling them they are eating the right thing. With severe larval infestations, the most reliable all-out attack is to poison them with sabadilla dust or rotenone.

To prevent future problems, keep track of emergence times in your garden and be especially vigilant patrolling for adults when they are expected to appear. Planting bush beans in alternate rows with potatoes seems to upset their egg-laying plans. Succession or timed planting can be a valuable strategy for working around this pest. In my Zone 7 garden, I get light infestations on spring beans, heavy damage to summer crops, and almost no bean beetle trouble in fall.

Several tiny wasps and flies parasitize Mexican bean beetle larvae, including well-known native predators. However, don't bother releasing purchased *Pediobius* or eulophid wasps unless you have more than one-quarter acre of infested beans. Although these two wasp species love to devour one of a gardener's most irritating visitors, they will quickly fly away if they don't find a banquet of bean beetle larvae in front of their noses.

Mosquitoes

Mosquitoes are included here not be-
cause they damage garden plants but because
they are such a nuisance to gardeners. In the
cool of the evening, when conditions are
perfect for weeding and harvesting, mosquitoes search us out, ready to suck blood from
any exposed bit of skin. Some people seem
more attractive to mosquitoes than others,
but none of us are immune to their sneaky

adult: ⅜"/10mm

and painful attacks. As if that weren't bad enough, mosquitoes spread many diseases and historically have posed more threats to human health than any other insect.

Several herbal oils repel mosquitoes, including citronella, wormwood, and pennyroyal. Instead of rubbing these oils (or hand-fuls of the plants themselves) on your skin, it's a better idea to treat a lightweight, long-sleeved shirt with one of these aromatic repellents and wear it during the hours when mosquitoes are most numerous.

Several common predators, including dragonflies, birds, frogs, and bats, eat mosquitoes. Purple martins are known for mosquito gluttony, but since they feed mostly during the day and mosqui-toes fly mostly at night, that reputation is probably exaggerated. Bats eat thousands of mosquitoes each week. You may see them in the evening sky, looking like small swallows as they dart through the air, eating mosquitoes.

If you have a still-water pond that serves so well as a mosquito nursery that natural predators cannot possibly keep them in check, there is a form of Bt (the *israelensis* strain, known as BTI) that can control mosquitoes in the larval stage. It doesn't work in fast-flowing water but may be of tremendous benefit in small ponds and lakes.

Nematodes

Nematodes, sometimes called eelworms, are not insects but microscopic worms that live in the soil. Most are decomposers; many are beneficial, as they live inside the bodies of cutworms and other soil-dwelling pests, causing them to die young. (See **Nematodes** in Chapter 5 for information on using beneficial nematodes.)

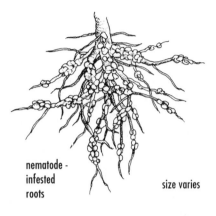

nematode - infested roots

size varies

Yet especially in warm climates, the southern root-knot nematode and other nematode species are horrible pests. These harmful nematodes enter plant roots, or even aboveground stems, and interfere with the plant's ability to take up water and nutrients. The root-knot nematode often creates small galls on plant roots.

When a plant is said to be nematode resistant, as with many hybrid tomatoes, that resistance is to the root-knot nematode. These nematodes thrive in sandy soil that seldom freezes in winter. They are most active in warm weather and often reach peak populations in late summer. Root-knot nematodes parasitize a number of garden crops. Okra, peppers, and most root crops are highly susceptible.

This pest occurs naturally in many soils, so getting rid of it once and for all is impractical. Rather, you must learn how to live with your nematodes. Nematode-control strategies include choosing resistant varieties, rotating susceptible crops with resistant ones, solarizing soil prior to planting fall root crops, and doing all you can to provide plants with ideal growing conditions and plenty of water.

Root-knot nematodes shun French marigolds, ryes and most other small grains, sweet potatoes, and members of the cabbage family. Growing one of these during the first half of the summer (or interplanting with marigolds) can reduce the number of nematodes present in fall.

In summer, soil solarization is accomplished by getting the soil ready for planting, wetting it down, and then covering it with a loose sheet of clear plastic for a month. The heat trapped under the plastic cooks the nematodes in the top few inches of soil. Do not recultivate the soil prior to planting with susceptible crops.

For long-term control, build up the organic matter in your soil to encourage predacious fungi. Also incorporate crab shells, shrimp hulls, eggshells, and other materials that contain chitin into your soil at every opportunity. This stimulates the proliferation of soil microorganisms that eat chitin. Since nematode eggs are covered with chitin, a lot of chitin-eating microcritters means fewer nematodes.

Onion Maggots

These nasty little creatures love cool, damp weather. Like many other flies, they overwinter as tiny pupae and emerge in spring. Eggs laid around onion plants hatch into wormy little maggots that devour all the underground parts of onions. If a maggot leaves one onion and squirms to a neighbor-

adult: ⅓"/9mm
larva: ⅓"/9mm

ing plant, the feeding wounds left behind may become infected with soilborne diseases.

Where this pest is common, lift all onions at season's end, even those that are perennial. Carefully sort and set aside any bulbs that may harbor maggots. Little brown "wheat berries" that fall from cull onions are probably pupae. With perennial bunching onions and potato onions, reset only clean, pest-free plants as far from the prior growing site as possible.

When growing bulb onions from seed, keep the seedbed covered with floating row covers. Transplant the seedlings to soil where onions were not grown before, and dust the furrow lightly with fresh wood ashes. You may sprinkle additional ashes on the surface, or you can use hot pepper powder to discourage the egg-laying flies. Since wet soil favors this pest, growing onions in well-drained raised beds can help limit damage. Where problems are epidemic, protect your onions throughout the growing season with floating row covers held aloft with hoops.

Parsley Worms, Celery Worms, or Carrot Worms

larva: 1¾" – 2"/4.5cm – 5.1cm

A voracious consumer of parsley, celery, dill, and carrot foliage, this creature is best known as the black swallowtail butterfly. It is an exception to the general rule that pretty butterflies don't damage garden plants. I have encountered this pest only once and thoroughly enjoyed our brief acquaintance. In midsummer, I noticed a dozen vividly colored green, black, and yellow caterpillars munching on a stand of parsley. (The green exactly matched the hue of the parsley.) When I picked one, it protested by thrusting forth a pair of bright orange fleshy horns. With the help of my young daughter and two of her friends, we discovered that if you let one of these caterpillars crawl on your arm and gently stroke its back, it can be counted on to show off its flamboyant, reputedly fragrant horns.

We installed the three biggest parsley worms in a gallon jar filled with parsley trimmings. We added several stout twigs for the worms to use when they were ready to create cocoons. The wait for metamorphosis was a short one, as butterflies emerged only two weeks after the caterpillars entered their pupal stage. It was a wonderful summertime adventure for the kids that I will certainly repeat when I get another chance.

These larvae may occasionally be so numerous on large plantings of parsley, celery, or carrots that handpicking is impractical. In that case, the definitive control agent is Bt, applied when the worms are young.

Pear Psylla

An old common name for these little insects is jumping plant lice. Pear psyllas are very small, less than one-eighth of an inch long when fully grown, and resemble miniature cicadas in that the psylla's wings are larger than the bodies.

H

adult: 1⁄10"/2.5mm

Pear psyllas overwinter in bark crevices and become active in early spring, just as the buds of dormant trees begin to swell. By the time pear flowers open, the psyllas are busy laying eggs on buds and in cracks in wood. Psylla nymphs feed by sucking sap from young leaves. They often become well established in neglected trees over a period of years. Heavy feeding year after year can seriously weaken infested trees.

A single dormant oil spray applied in early spring, just before buds swell, usually brings this pest under control. In addition, many of the beneficial insects that feed on aphids also attack pear psyllas, including lady beetle larvae, tiny wasps, and lacewing larvae.

Pill Bugs

This creature has many names, including pill bug, sow bug, wood louse, and roly-poly. It is not really an insect, but a crustacean, a primitive relation of the crayfish and crab. Like its cousins, it works as a scavenger, living among and devouring dead plant material. Pill bugs love dark, damp places such as compost heaps, the inside corners of cold frames, and greenhouse floors.

adult: 3⁄8"/10mm

Whether or not pill bugs are garden pests is open to debate. On occasion, they will feed on young seedlings, but they seldom damage older plants. Should they become destructive, you can easily trap them by placing pieces of a decaying fruit or vegetable beneath a flowerpot turned upside down. Early in the morning, collect the bugs from beneath the trap and kill them by dropping them into a pail of very hot water. Or you can transport them to the woods and set them free.

Keep in mind that pill bugs are not a pest simply because they are present. My climate is rich in pill bugs, but I have never felt compelled to kill a single one. They are quite numerous in the composting area, where I suspect they aid substantially in the decomposition of vegetable matter. Children love to play with them, as they roll up into a ball when disturbed, then make quite a show of tickling a small hand or arm as they desperately try to scuttle to freedom.

Plum Curculios

adult: ¼"/6mm

Peach, cherry, plum, and apple trees are prey to this tiny, determined insect. The adults feed on tender buds, blossoms, and green fruits of trees just after they have finished blooming. The females cut crescent-shaped punctures as they lay their eggs in the green fruits, and the fruits are thus disfigured. When the eggs hatch, the grubs feed inside the fruits. After feeding for two to three weeks, they drop to the ground and pupate, and a second generation emerges.

Adult curculios often are called snout beetles because they, like other weevils, have such elaborate mouthparts. Although quite small, they can be present in large numbers, especially in trees growing near woodland areas. The adults overwinter in bark crevices, beneath logs and stones, and in other natural shelter present in woods.

There are several ways to outwit this insect. One is to allow hens to feed on the ground below fruit trees. Chickens are so adept at pecking curculios that some people plant plums in the chicken yard.

In early summer, when fruit trees thin themselves by dropping some of their green fruits, pick up the fallen fruits promptly. Many of them may harbor the first generation of curculio larvae (or **codling moth** larvae — see page 47).

Another method of control depends on the curious curculio habit of playing dead when disturbed. In the cool of the morning, place sheets beneath trees and knock limbs vigorously with a stick, one at a time. Many adult curculios will fall to the ground, where you can quickly gather them up, then dump them in a bucket of very hot water. They can fly, so work quickly.

Plum curculios have several natural enemies that may be harmed by the use of organic pesticides. However, if many of the fallen green fruits show evidence of curculio damage, you may wish to use pyrethrin or rotenone the following season to rid the trees of this pest. These pesticides are only effective on adults before fruits form, not on the larvae inside green fruits.

Praying Mantises

adult: 2½" – 3"/6.4cm – 7.6cm

Praying mantises are so spectacular that they tend to receive plenty of publicity. A textbook example of a good insect that eats no plants, only other insects, the pray-ing mantis is often hailed as the best living thing you can find in a garden.

Although the mantis is indeed a friend, its good deeds prob-ably are exaggerated. The problem is that the mantis is a delicate being, with no defense other than camouflage to safeguard it from birds, snakes, and other animals for which it makes a nice break-fast. This situation is aggravated by the fact that only one genera-tion per year is the norm, a very limiting factor in the mantis's population possibilities.

Watching a praying mantis hunt is better than any science fiction movie. As you approach, the head turns quizzically to ex-amine you. Stand still, and the mantis will turn its attention back to its vigil, ultimately pouncing with sudden speed on an unsus-pecting victim. This goes on day and night in trees, bushes, and grasses.

Praying mantises overwinter as eggs within stiff gray or brown egg cases, which are usually left attached to twigs on trees, shrubs, and bushes. The little mantises hatch in late spring and carry on their good deeds in such small ways that we seldom notice them until late summer. By then they have grown quite large, and violent matings have resulted in the survival of mostly big, fertile females. Enjoying the companionship of these green ladies is one of the gardener's rewards for not using toxic pesticides in the garden. Like many other large beneficial insects, praying mantises are easily killed by contact with poisons.

To increase the number of mantises that inhabit your property, plant bushes near the garden. You might also consider planting a beneficial hedge down the center of a large row-type garden so that mantises (and dozens of other helpful species) will have a fixed, season-long habitat. If you see any wild, naturally occurring mantises in your immediate area, resist the temptation to import store-bought populations. Introduced strains may give the natives too much competition, and you can rest assured that your yard's ancestral strain of mantis is the one best equipped to thrive for many generations to come.

Raspberry Cane Borers

adult: ⅓"/9mm

Two different insects cause swollen galls to form near the tips of raspberry canes, and sometimes on roses. Both are small beetles whose larvae are borers that feed inside the canes. Before you see the swelling on a cane, you will probably notice some wilting of leaves growing on the cane's tip. You also may notice one or two rings of tiny punctures around the stem. When such wilting occurs, find the row of punctures or the weak and swollen section of stem, prune it off below the gall, and destroy it. Later in summer, go back and look for additional galls and prune them off as well. If you manage to intercept this pest one summer, it is unlikely to reappear for several seasons unless your raspberry collection is quite large.

Robber Flies

An ugly ally, the robber fly often haunts home gardens. A mighty predator of all sorts of insects, this fly is similar to the common housefly,

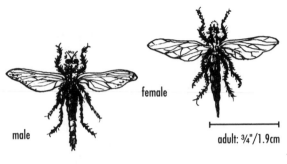

female

male

adult: ¾"/1.9cm

except that its hairy body is long and tapered, often ending in a point. That pointed rear end is nothing compared to the sharp mouthparts it uses to bite and consume insects both smaller and larger that itself. Robber flies can be frightening at times, as some grow to be more than an inch long.

The robber fly is a loud buzzer. It probably got its name from the way it pounces on prey. The larvae also are predators, often eating small beetle larvae they find in leaf piles and compost heaps.

You don't have to do anything special to encourage this insect, as it usually finds all it needs in the varied plants and fixtures of a diversified home garden.

Rose Chafers

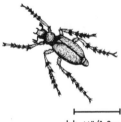

adult: ½"/1.3cm

If you grow roses or grapes near a lawn or other grassy area, you are likely to see these long-legged light brown beetles skeletonizing leaves and eating blossoms. The damage looks similar to that done by the Japanese beetle, but the rose chafer is easily identified by its smaller size, lighter color, and much longer legs. In addition to roses and grapes, the chafer feeds on fruit trees, leafy greens, and most small fruits, including strawberries, blackberries, and raspberries.

The close proximity of a lawn affects rose chafer populations, for this beetle spends most of the year as a small white grub, feeding on grass roots six inches underground. Frequent cultivation helps to control the beetles in large orchards. In most backyards, plowing up your lawn is not practical.

To keep resident populations from becoming established, handpick these beetles whenever you find them. Drop them in a jar of soapy water, screw on the lid, and wait until the beetles are dead. Then remove the lid and set the jars of decomposing beetles among roses and grapes. The close presence (or smell) of these corpses may deter feeding by other beetles. When infestations are very severe and beetles are eating every grape blossom in sight, a timely application of rotenone may be needed.

Scale

adult: ⅛"/3.2mm

Scale insects come in many colors and forms, but all cling to stems and twigs so tightly that they look like tiny seashells. Thus ensconced on a plant, they suck its juices and weaken the plant. Most scale insects produce sticky honeydew, which supports black fungal deposits called sooty mold.

Scale is most often seen on houseplants and fruit trees, and occasionally on other crops. On houseplants, you may rub the little insects off with your fingers or touch them lightly with a cotton swab dipped in alcohol. Houseplants that host scale may be set outside in late spring, and natural predators may take care of the problem.

Small congregations of scale on fruit-tree twigs also may be removed by hand, or you can use a sponge or soft brush and soapy water. Pay special attention to the undersides of twigs, where scale tend to gather. The colonies look like tiny shell-covered bumps. When you're pruning, remove small limbs that hold clusters of scale and burn them. In late winter, dormant oil applied to leafless fruit trees will suffocate most types of scale. When citrus fruits become ridden with scale, use the form of horticultural oil known as summer oil or sun oil to control them even while the plants are not dormant but are covered with green leaves. Just be sure to use the right type of oil, which is different from the earlier forms of dormant oil.

Slugs and Snails

Slimy moving lumps that leave a shiny trail behind them are slugs. Slugs with shells on their backs are snails; both are mollusks rather than insects. If your garden hosts but a few of these creatures, you don't have a problem. However, if damp weather combines with a suitable habitat, your garden can quickly become so thick with slugs and

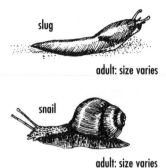

slug

adult: size varies

snail

adult: size varies

snails that no leafy green is left unslimed and every strawberry is ruined as soon as it blushes pink.

There are many ways to get rid of slugs, but all slug-fighting strategies should begin with an understanding of their habits. Slugs feed at night and hide in leaves and beneath boards and rocks during the day. If your vegetable garden is very close to a deck (where slugs lurk during the day), or if your compost area is at the garden's edge (a too-attractive place from a slug's point of view), you will be constantly fighting against them. Besides changing the layout of your yard, you can limit its slug allure by keeping the lower branches of bushes pruned so that your shrubs do not become sheltered slug castles.

Perhaps the oldest slug remedy is salt, which dehydrates slugs when you sprinkle it on them. Slug salting is best done by hand because it's important to limit the amount of salt that ends up in the soil. Forgo salt altogether if you live in a desert area where salt accumulation in soil is already a problem. Instead, handpick the slugs or spear them with a fork, then dump them into a jar of salty water. Wear rubber gloves to make slug gathering less slimy.

Several substances make effective slug and snail barriers when sprinkled in a ring around plants or beds. Diatomaceous earth, lime, and fresh sawdust work well, although you will need to replace these barriers after every rain.

Many gardeners trap and dispose of slugs using shallow dishes filled with beer or half-buried tin cans baited with vegetable or fruit trimmings. To be effective, these traps must be checked and emptied periodically and reset at night. Boards laid out between rows often attract slugs, as they provide good daytime shelter. Again, the slugs lurking there must be collected and disposed of frequently, or they will be back every night to range through the garden.

Where slug populations are extremely high, some gardeners use strips of copper as collars around beds. For some reason, slugs will not cross copper. Though relatively expensive, long copper strips are one of the best slug-control measures.

Soldier Bugs

The soldier bug looks much like a common stink bug, or may be mistaken for a squash bug (although squash bugs are longer and more slender). To be certain that you are looking at a soldier bug, look for its sharp, spinelike shoulders, which stink bugs and squash bugs do not have. The slightly speckled blackish bugs are active all summer.

adult: ½"/1.3cm

A very young soldier bug will sip plant juices, but as it becomes older it uses its probiscus to consume the insides of soft-bodied caterpillars, Mexican bean beetle larvae, and several other common pests. Gather and kill squash bugs and stink bugs, but not the soldier, with its distinctive epaulets on its shoulders.

Spiders

By some estimates, more than ten thousand spiders may inhabit a rural acre on a summer day. Most are seldom seen. Despite having eight eyes, most spiders can't see well and depend on their trapping skills to feed themselves.

black widow spider

Spiders will trap and kill just about any insect they can sink their tiny fangs into.

size varies

Those fangs are laced with venom, which slowly paralyze the spider's victim. The spider then moves in and feeds on the juicy insides of its prey. Since spiders are limited to this semiliquid diet, they must kill numerous insects.

Clearly, spiders are helpful creatures, and we must go out of our way to protect them. When a spider scurries away as we till, trying to roll her egg sac along with her, pause to accommodate her escape. Although it may seem to the fastidious housekeeper that spiders have too many babies, in fact many reproduce less vigorously than true insects. Spiders also are highly sensitive to pesticides.

Will spiders bite you? Some may make that mistake, but not the hairy little jumping spiders often seen pouncing on smaller insects in the garden. Jumping spiders can see better than species that trap their prey in webs, and they probably recognize large animals such as humans for what they are. To spiders, we are not attractive prey.

Poisonous spiders are quite rare, and the only one you are likely to encounter near a garden is the black widow. She will not be among garden plants. Every summer I find at least one black widow somewhere in my yard, usually beneath a rock or in some other spot sheltered from rain. I kill them with boiling water.

As for the big garden spiders often seen among shrubs and perennial flowers, do what you can to preserve their habitat from year to year. Some live to be three years old, but they will not survive without year-round shelter. Birds and frogs eat spiders. In a vegetable garden, leave a hedge or bed of cover crop plants standing through the winter to give spiders a protected habitat when they need it most.

Spider Mites

It's a good thing that spider mites are so small. Otherwise, we would likely be overwhelmed by the sheer number of this common, widely distributed pest. The mites that are most injurious to plants, the red and two-spotted spider mites, turn up on flowers, vegetables, shrubs, and fruit trees as soon as the weather turns hot in midsummer.

adult:
less than ⅟₅₀"/.5mm

Gardeners often are advised to get a magnifying glass and examine the undersides of leaves to find spider mites, but such a search may end in frustration. If the infestation is very severe, you may see nearly invisible dots hidden under the sheerest of webbing, but then again you may see nothing at all. So instead of looking for the pest, look for its symptoms. The leaves of plants overrun with spider mites will be ashen light green, with thousands of tiny yellow speckles that run together to give the leaves a bleached appearance.

Weather and spider mite populations are closely tied together. Under warm, dry conditions, spider mites multiply rapidly, so much so that ten or more generations may pass in the course of the summer. Eggs hatch in only three days, and the time span from egg to adult may be as short as one week.

Fortunately, spider mites have a number of natural enemies that often manage to keep them under control, especially in mild climates. Predatory mites (which can be purchased for mite control in greenhouses), lady beetles, thrips, and many other little bugs devour spider mites.

However, even a legion of natural predators often proves insufficient in areas with a warm, dry summer (or indoors). The situation is made worse by the fact that problems are difficult or impossible to discover until they are well under way and the mites number in the millions.

You may need to use several strategies. If spider mites are a common pest in your garden, appearing year after year, prepare for them in advance. Spray fruit trees with dormant oil in late winter to eliminate eggs of European red mites. In spring, treat flowers, shrubs, and berries with a soap spray as soon as they leaf out, and repeat the spraying every week as needed throughout the summer.

Spider mites greatly dislike being doused with water, so if mites are epidemic in your area, it's a good idea to wet the foliage when watering plants. Be sure to do this late in the day, when the water on plant leaves will not heat up and leave burn spots behind.

In my climate, spider mites tend to appear in small pockets on neighboring plants. When I see their telltale damage, I treat plants with a spray made from soap and citrus peels. This has some impact, but the most dramatic results have occurred when I have then covered the plants with an old blanket for three days. The cover keeps the plants cool and moist — just the type of environment spider mites detest. I follow up with a second spray on the fourth or fifth day after the first treatment, and soon I see new leaves emerging that are not marred by yellow pinpricks.

Squash Bugs

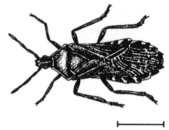

adult: ½"/1.3cm

One of the few true bugs that bother garden plants, squash bugs are a widespread pest of summer and winter squash. For some reason, they often prefer zucchini, although they will proliferate on any type of squash if given a chance. Pumpkins, melons, and cucumbers sometimes become involved, too.

Adult squash bugs overwinter in weeds, tree bark, woodpiles, and buildings. They emerge in spring and usually manage to find squash just as it begins to grow well. Early in summer, if you look beneath the lowest leaves and around the basal stem, you are likely to find a few specimens to collect. Later in the season, spray plants with water to get the bugs moving. They will run to the undersides of leaves or drop to the ground, where they are easy to handpick.

You may remove clusters of oval, orange to brown squash-bug eggs by rubbing the leaves gently with your fingers. The ugly little nymphs that hatch (after about ten days) pierce and suck from leaves with sharp mouthparts. The nymphs are sometimes parasitized by small flies and wasps.

If handpicking does not adequately control this pest, watch closely to see whether one or two plants are more severely infested than others. Cover these with an old sheet, pull them up, and remove them from the garden. Alternatively, dust plants with sabadilla or rotenone to poison the squash bugs. Cover treated plants with sheets or floating row covers for two days after treatment to keep honeybees and other beneficials from coming into contact with these poisons. Nasturtiums planted among squash may help repel squash bugs.

Squash Vine Borers

adult: 1" – 1½"/2.5cm – 3.8cm

This heartbreaking pest is difficult to spot until damage to squash plants is well under way. The adult is a moth that looks more like a large black-and-red elongated fly or wasp. In late spring or early summer, the moth lays its eggs on the lower stems of squash plants, and occasionally on pumpkin, gourd,

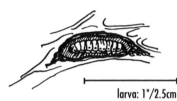

larva: 1"/2.5cm

cucumber, or muskmelon plants as well. When the tiny eggs hatch, the emerging borers enter the stems and begin feeding inside. At this point, you may find a small hole in the lower stem surrounded by sawdustlike frass. As feeding continues, the portion of the plant beyond the borer will gradually wilt and die.

Because the borers damage plants from the inside, they are difficult to treat. Some gardeners slit open affected stems and fish out the borers with tweezers, but this surgery causes substantial trauma to the plants. I have had some success injecting liquid Bt into infested stems. Preventing egg laying by keeping squash plants covered with floating row covers until female flowers appear is the best defense. Female flowers have a distinctive bulge between flower and stem that is absent in males. Frequently female flowers do not appear until a week or two after the first males. Male flowers furnish pollen, but they cannot set fruit.

Butternut squash seldom has problems with borers, but all summer squash (and winter squash of the *Cucurbita pepo* species) are highly susceptible. Varieties with long vines that develop supplemental roots may continue to grow and flower despite borer damage to the plants' primary crowns. Timed planting also can help, as the borers are less likely to appear on squash grown in late summer and fall.

Symphylans

This root-eating pest is not a true insect, but in the Northwest where it is established, it is definitely a nuisance. Symphylans look like miniature white centipedes, only half an inch long, with long antennae. They look like little root hairs, but you can identify them by pulling up an infested plant and plunging the root into a bucket of water. If symphylans are present, they will float to the top.

Symphylan feeding is heaviest on young seedlings. They often bypass carrots, peas, and lettuce but ruin young plantings of cabbage and many other vegetable crops.

There are several ways to manage symphylan problems. The oldest remedy is to flood the garden with water and keep it flooded for a month in winter or two weeks in summer. So many symphylans drown that a good flooding can control them for more than a year.

If flooding is impractical, planting a cover crop right before you plant susceptible crops can help. Symphylans like tender young roots and may be repelled by large amounts of fresh green material in the soil. Water copiously after the green manure is turned under.

Heavy manuring right before planting also discourages symphylans. Use fresh manure and water it in very well prior to planting. Nitrogen burning from fresh manure may give plants a little trouble, but not as much as they would get from symphylans.

Syrphid Flies, Hover Flies

Also known as the hover fly or flowerfly, the syrphid fly nearly rivals the lady beetle in its appetite for aphids. Wherever plant health is threatened by aphids or the bothersome diseases they often carry, native populations of syrphid flies are deputies of natural law and order.

adult: ½"/1.3cm

Here's what they do. The females find plants with aphids on them, lay an egg or two in each aphid colony, and then pause and refresh themselves by grazing among the flowers. Within days, the eggs that survive (even beneficials have natural enemies) hatch into larvae. These larvae immediately start sticking their mouths into aphids and sucking them dry. Syrphid larvae have been observed killing one aphid per minute in this way.

Will they sting you? No, but they could be mistaken for sweat bees, which might. Sweat bees are small, true bees attracted to the salt in sweat and capable of relatively minor stings. Several other insects look like syrphid flies, including yellow jackets and bald-faced hornets. The syrphid is smaller, and its body is held straight out in contrast to the curled posture of the hornets. In addition, the syrphid fly hovers, suspended in midair, as it investigates its surroundings. Syrphids also spend more time around flowers than do stinging hornets.

For positive identification that the insects hovering around your hat are syrphids, catch a few in a jar with rubbing alcohol (to knock them out) and look at them carefully under a magnifying glass. In addition to their conspicuous and continuous hovering behavior, syrphids have only one set of wings, and their heads are quite large compared to their bodies. The syrphid's underbelly is usually a light solid color, but exact markings vary among native species. Certainly the fact that they look dangerous at first glance has helped earn syrphids their commanding place in the insect world.

Tachinid Flies

Tachinids are big, ugly, and cruel, but they are one of nature's best insurance agents when it comes to safeguarding plants from epidemics involving armyworms, corn borers, and gypsy moths. Tachinids look like large, hairy houseflies.

adult: ⅜"/10mm

Under normal circumstances, when the plant and animal life in the garden is well balanced and no pests are particularly troublesome, tachinids are seen flying about purposefully, checking out flowers and resting on plant leaves. Their purpose is grisly indeed.

Tachinid flies may lay eggs in front of a caterpillar so the caterpillar will eat them, or they may deposit live newborn larvae where they think a host is hiding. In these and other sneaky ways, the tachinid manages to get her maggots inside suitable hosts, where they feed and grow along with the host. Then, just as the host nears maturity, the tachinid maggot finishes it off and emerges to live a long and useful life.

When a fine reproductive opportunity presents itself, as when armyworms or other prey become especially numerous, tachinid flies promptly take advantage of the situation. In years when gypsy moths, armyworms, or corn borers are bad, expect to see many of these robust flies buzzing about.

Tarnished Plant Bugs

adult: ¼"/6mm

A wide-ranging enemy of most fruit and vegetable crops, the tarnished plant bug has the unpleasant ability to inject toxins into leaves and stems as it feeds. This can lead to unusual discolored dark spots on strawberry, celery, chard, beets, and related plants, which are probably its favorite foods. A true bug with a round back and tiny head, the tarnished plant bug is usually green to brown with darker markings on its back. Young tarnished plant bugs are green and gain coloration as they mature.

Finding tarnished plant bugs can be difficult, as the small bugs are quite shy and run for cover when plants are disturbed. If you manage to find one or two on a troubled plant, there probably are many more hidden within the leaves of neighboring plants.

Sabadilla dust easily kills tarnished plant bugs; it should be applied in the cool of the morning before the bugs are active. Because this insect overwinters in tree bark or weed debris near gardens and seldom travels very far, good control one year often will eliminate problems the following season. By the same token, a few tarnished plant bugs one year may precede a larger outbreak the next year. If a resident population is well established, grow susceptible crops under floating row covers.

Tent Caterpillars

This leaf-eating, colony-forming caterpillar has a strong preference for wild cherry and plum trees, although it will set up nests in apple, peach, and shade trees from time to time. The tent caterpillar is easy to identify because the little hairy worms spin

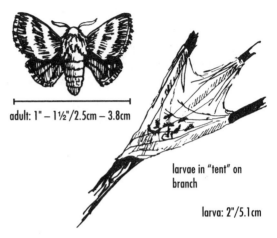

adult: 1" – 1½"/2.5cm – 3.8cm

larvae in "tent" on branch

larva: 2"/5.1cm

a webby tent around themselves, where they live in cozy comfort in early spring. Similar nests that appear in fall are the work of the fall webworm.

Tent caterpillars gather in their nests at night and during stormy weather. On nice days, they move out to devour massive amounts of leaves. The tents are usually suspended within the crotches of branches. To capture a whole tentful of these worms, attach a brush to the end of a long stick or drive several nails into the end of a long wooden pole. Spin and swirl this device around within the nest. Then use smaller sticks to scrape the tent off and drop it into a fire. Worms left without the protection of a nest may attempt to build a new one, or they may be snapped up by birds and other predators.

While you're wandering through the fruit orchard in winter, watch for the egg masses of this pest, which look like shiny dark brown blobs encircling twigs. Prune these off and burn them.

Like most leaf-eating caterpillars, tent caterpillars have many natural enemies that help to keep them under control. If small colonies are so high up in tree branches that you cannot reach them, take comfort in the fact that birds, wasps, and many other predators may take care of the problem for you.

Termites

The termite is not a pest of garden plants, but it is often found near gardens in wooden cold frames, posts, or the timbers that enclose raised beds. Termites should not be allowed to flourish close to a home, as they may secretly begin chewing on the wooden parts of your house's foundation, potentially causing thousands of dollars in damage.

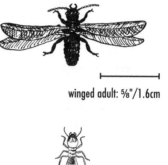

winged adult: ⅝"/1.6cm

The termite looks like an ant except that it lacks the ant's thin waist.

worker adult: ¼"/6mm

The young and worker adults are wingless beige creatures found in cavities they have eaten in pieces of wood. They must have contact with the soil and usually build earthen tunnels to connect themselves with the ground. Destroying the tunnel can interrupt the life of the colony, but it's also a good idea to douse the area with boiling water. If you find termites in the wooden structures in your garden, closely inspect the foundation of your house to see whether earthen tunnels are present. Professional guidance is called for if your house has become a haven for termites.

Thrips

Thrips are so small that they are very difficult to see. But if you leave a bouquet of daisies on your kitchen table and a number of tiny creatures fall down when you tap the blossoms, you are viewing flower thrips. A similar creature sometimes feeds on young onions in the vegetable garden. Rather than

adult: less than ¹⁄₂₅"/1mm

seeing the thrips themselves, you will see whitish patches on the onion leaves, indicating that thrips have been feeding.

Thrips are so small that they often blow in with the wind, surprising the gardener with their presence. In the South, they carry and transmit tomato spotted wilt virus and may carry other viruses to other plants as well.

It is difficult or impossible to fight an enemy that you cannot see, so the best defense against thrips is to grow healthy plants. You can manage thrips on fruit trees with dormant oil applied in winter. On onions and other vegetables, insecticidal soap or aromatic herbal sprays with soap added will slow down thrip damage, as will destroying severely infested plants.

Tomato Fruitworms

See **Corn Earworms.**

Tomato Hornworms

See **Hornworms.**

Trichogramma Wasps

adult: less than ⅟₂₅"/1mm

These minute wasps are only specks when fully grown. Their tiny size and tawny yellow color make them very hard to see and facilitate the work they do in gardens. Other little beneficial wasps parasitize larvae, but this one lays its eggs in other insects' eggs. The trichogramma eggs hatch almost immediately, the larvae feed inside the host egg, and new adults emerge in only two or three weeks. Blackened or vacant eggs are often the only clue that trichogrammas are at work.

Trichogrammas may be purchased and released, but they are expensive and will do little good except in large areas where a huge supply of moth eggs is waiting for them. Wild trichogrammas live throughout the United States and may be encouraged by growing plenty of flowers that produce small blossoms and severely limiting your use of pesticides, including botanical (natural) types.

Wasps, Hornets

adult: ¾"/1.9cm

All gardeners must somehow learn to tolerate and accept wasps, which are found in any climate warm enough to support a garden. Some species are sold as beneficial predators; see **Braconid Wasps** (page 42), **Ichneumon Wasps** (page 67), and **Trichogramma Wasps** (page 97). In general, gardeners will encounter two types of wasps: the large, thin-waisted paper wasp, which builds small honeycombed colonies in barns, outbuildings, and beneath the eaves of houses, and the yellow jacket, which usually nests in the ground and is a frightful creature indeed.

Paper wasps are seldom interested in stinging people unless their nests are threatened. To keep out of their way, you may need to watch porches and window frames vigilantly in early summer to make sure they are not attempting to nest there. A single female or two building a small nest may give way to a much larger nest by midsummer. Scare the first nest builders away with a strong stream of water, then scrape off the nest with a stiff broom. If the wasps return and resume their work, pyrethrum spray will kill them.

You do not want to kill every wasp you see, for they are important predators of caterpillars. Paper wasps and yellow jackets feed their young protein-rich bug meat and are clearly beneficial insects. However, if you have too many wasps around your house, step on the large ones seen stretching their legs on chilly mornings in fall and early spring. These are usually fertile females that will become colony queens in early summer.

Yellow jackets are more vicious than paper wasps. When their nests are even slightly disturbed, large numbers will fly from the underground hole to attack the enemy with painful stings. Gardeners often discover these nests by accident, while mowing neglected areas or weeding around trees. Run when you see a number of "bees" the size of honeybees, only brighter in color and less hairy, coming and going from a hole in the ground. Avoid the area until you can go out at dawn on a very cool morning and douse the hole with boiling water. Don't assume that the nest is gone after one treatment.

A few other hornets may be common around homes and gardens. Mud daubers are wasps that build long tubes for their young; they attach these to porches, wood chairs, and other wooden structures. However, they do not hang around to protect them and pose no danger to humans. The hornets that build big nests shaped like roundish cones do protect their communities. Do not allow these predominantly black hornets, called bald-faced hornets, to begin building a nest attached to your house. If one is established and hangs from a tree limb near your yard, stay away from it and try to tolerate its presence until winter, when it can safely be removed. If you threaten a colony of bald-faced hornets, they will threaten you back.

Weevils

Weevils of beans and southern peas (cowpeas) are the main reason home gardeners have such a difficult time growing quality dry beans for storage. Adult weevils are so small that they often pass unnoticed. H

adult: 1/10" – 1/4"/2.5mm – 6mm

If you catch a small snout beetle among your beans that looks like a plum curculio, you have found a weevil. All are members of the same huge and diversified insect family.

Secretively, bean and pea weevils lay their eggs on pods or manage to get locked inside the pods at flowering. One way or the other, they get their young into developing legume seeds, where the larvae slowly feed. Many an unsuspecting gardener has laboriously grown, picked, threshed, and stored dry beans or peas, only to find them riddled with holes and little worms within weeks after they are placed in storage.

Because weevils are so good at what they do, in some areas it is just not practical to grow beans for dry storage. You can, however, grow beans for freezing even where weevils are common. If shell beans are picked when still somewhat green and then blanched well before freezing, any eggs or tiny larvae present will be killed and are seldom seen in the frozen beans.

If you suspect that your beans are free of weevils, it's still a good idea to subject them to heat and freezing temperatures before storing them. Lay the cleaned beans in a shallow pan and place them in a 175°F (80°C) oven for an hour. When the beans are cool, bag them and freeze them for a week. These temperature changes will kill any hidden weevils, and you can then store the beans at room temperature.

You can reduce weevil problems in the garden by sowing beans very early, before weevils are moving about, and promptly turning under the plants after harvest.

Whiteflies

H
adult: ⅒"/2.5mm

The whitefly is yet another very tiny insect that can do quite a bit of damage. Many species of whiteflies are common in North America, but they usually don't cause problems in small home gardens filled with a number of different plants. Natural predators often keep them under control. They are rarely problematic except in warm climates and greenhouses (and on indoor plants), where they can reproduce a dozen times in the course of a year.

All whiteflies are very tiny creatures that resemble a cross between an aphid and a moth. They tend to congregate in large numbers. When disturbed, a cloud of the gnatlike flies may flutter in the air. Larvae feed on leaf undersides and give off honeydew, which leads to the proliferation of sooty mold, a black fungus.

In the Southwest, the sweet potato whitefly carries a terrible squash virus that has become so widespread that floating row covers are needed to protect this crop. In citrus-growing areas, citrus trees in home gardens often need to be sprayed with insecticidal soap to eliminate whiteflies. In greenhouses, whiteflies can be brought under control permanently by releasing the tiny parasitic wasp *Encarsia formosa.*

Wireworms

The adult form of this insect, the click beetle, is so entertaining that one must partially forgive the larva, known as the wireworm, for its awesome appetite for potatoes and corn. Catch a few click beetles — slender, tawny brown beetles that sometimes slip indoors — and turn them on their backs. Then watch them right themselves by snapping the strong hinge between their two thorax segments. You will see why they have earned the name click beetle, as well as nicknames such as skipjack and snap bug.

adult: ½"/1.3cm

larva: 1"/2.5cm

What the larvae do below ground is in no way amusing. The long orange worms with bodies that appear jointed (and unusually shiny for a subterranean creature) burrow into potatoes, flower bulbs, and the roots of corn and other vegetables. Some wireworms feed for several years before becoming adults. Both adult beetles and their larvae are resident insects that seldom travel far from home.

There are two wonderfully specific ways to deal with this pest. First, set vegetable traps, using potato pieces as bait, five inches below ground where wireworms are present. See page 129 for instructions for making wireworm traps from tin cans.

A second strategy is to attract and collect mature adults. Click beetles like sweet, sticky syrups, such as corn syrup and molasses, which can be dribbled on fence posts or stout wood stakes. Gather beetles found sipping the syrup. Don't lace your lures with poison, or you may kill innocent honeybees, wasps, and butterflies.

◀ CHAPTER 5 ▶

Remedies, Recipes, and Formulas
for Earth-Safe Insect Control

*In this strange attitude the Mantis stands motionless, with
eyes fixed on her prey. If the Locust moves, the Mantis turns
her head. The object of this performance is plain. It is intended to strike terror into the heart of the victim, to paralyse
it with fright before attacking it. The Mantis is pretending to
be a Ghost! The plan is quite successful.*

Jean-Henri Fabre
Souveniers Entomologiques

When we got a new blender to replace the one that started shoot-
ing sparks, my husband made me promise not to puree bugs in the
new one. "I don't do that anymore," I protested. "It doesn't work."
Indeed, bug juice is but one of several natural pest-control remedies that have fallen out of favor because they promised more
than they delivered. I'll try anything once — even gathering,
liquefying, straining, and spraying bug corpses. Actually, I tried
that one three times, using three different species of insects. The
greatest benefit of my bug juice teas was the handpicking I did to
obtain ingredients.

At the same time, the bug juices did no harm to my plants or
to the environment, so they can be properly classified as harmless.
Yet a few decades ago, when gardeners were scrambling to find
ways to control insects other than using toxic pesticides, they
embraced some methods of questionable ecological integrity.

Blenders were used not only to puree bug bodies but to mix kerosene and soap (to spray on insect eggs). Soot scraped from the inside walls of chimneys was thrown on caterpillars.

These days, few of us wish to use kerosene in our gardens, and hopefully everyone who scrapes sooty creosote from chimneys wears gloves and a dust mask (the particles are carcinogenic). Just because a pest-control method is old does not make it safe — for either the environment or us. The recipes in this chapter are harmless when properly made and applied. When trying any novel formula, stop and give careful thought to its effect on the local environment before proceeding.

Some pest-control measures from long ago, such as arsenic and DDT, are best forgotten in the name of safety. But there are plenty of new ideas and practices to take their places. The following list includes forty-three recipes and methods for controlling garden insects, including many of very recent invention. Along with the formulas, I've given a brief explanation of how the substances work. When using any pest-control remedy, think about how the desired result will be achieved. If the process involves innocent casualties of nontarget insects, as when honeybees and other beneficials are accidentally killed by potent botanical pesticides, you may want to find a solution that's less dangerous to the balance of life in your garden. Or you can cover plants with blankets or row covers after they are treated to keep good bugs from wandering into the killing zone.

Following is an alphabetical list of pest remedies; sources for purchasing those predators and products that aren't homemade are listed in Appendix A. Metric equivalents for measurements in the formulas are given in Appendix C.

Alcohol

Isopropyl or rubbing alcohol is handy for controlling mealybugs and scale on houseplants and small, waxy-leafed shrubs. However, care must be taken not to get alcohol on plant leaves, for it will burn them. The best approach is to dampen a cotton swab or small cotton ball with alcohol and dab or wipe it on the pests. Repeat after two weeks if problems continue.

Aromatic Herbs

The list of aromatic herbs that you can use in your battles with garden insects is a long one, and it can be simple and exciting to try different combinations as pest-control remedies. Just as we experience riveting olfactory stimulation from aromatic herbs, insects may be confused or disgusted when they sense the presence of mints on muskmelons or rosemary on tomatoes.

Many insects, especially moths and butterflies, wear their noses on their feet. They sense whether they have found a good host plant by walking around on it. It stands to reason that if you coat plant leaves with the essence of an alien plant, these insects may mistake an attractive one for another that they do not recognize or like.

Some of the best herbs for making sprayable teas include wormwood, mints, lavender, rosemary, sage, tansy (see **Tansy,** page 127), and southernwood. Pungent herb seeds, including dill, anise,

A Word About Wormwood

The hardy perennial herb known as wormwood or absinthe (Artemisia absinthium) *is but one type of artemisia you may want to grow in your garden. Its gray-green leaves are very pungent and widely recommended for repelling fleas, moths, and other small insects. My dog may have discovered this on her own a few summers back, as her favorite resting spot in the garden was beneath a robust wormwood bush. A few other artemisias smell better to human noses and are pretty enough for the flower border. These include southernwood (A. abrotanum), French tarragon (A. dracunculus), and low-growing 'Silver mound' (A. schmidtiana) and Roman wormwood (A. pontica).*

and fennel, may give herbal bug sprays extra punch.

To make herb sprays with fresh herbs, take a large bunch of leaves and stems, crush them well with your hands (the fun part), and place them in a small heat-proof container. Pour a quart of boiling water over the herbs, stir well, and allow to cool. Strain the tea through a metal strainer, then through muslin or another fine cloth if many particles remain in the tea (they may clog up the head of your spray bottle). Add two drops of mild liquid soap and decant the tea into a pump spray bottle. Apply the spray to plants early in the morning, before the sun shines brightly and just before most insects begin their daily activities.

You can use dried herbs to make bug-deterrent teas by infusing the herbs with boiling water. To make sure dried herbs retain their aroma, dry them quickly in summer, when the weather is warm, and store them in airtight containers in a cool, dark place until you need them. Label containers clearly, especially when saving inedible herbs such as wormwood.

Teas made from aromatic herbs are good first aid remedies for many different bug-ridden plants, and growing herbs in the vegetable garden, interspersed with food crops, is a prime measure for preventing pest problems. Besides confusing bugs as they search for host plants, many herbs bear small flowers that attract little wasps and other beneficial insects. Herbs that grow into large perennials, such as wormwood and hardy strains of rosemary, also provide shelter and habitat for larger beneficials, such as spiders and praying mantises. Instead of locating your herb garden in a separate part of your yard, give it a prominent place in the food garden. In this way, your collection of herbs becomes a year-round haven for predators and a party place for small beneficial insects that dine on various plant-eating bugs.

Bacillus thuringiensis, Bt

Usually known simply as Bt, *Bacillus thuringiensis* is a bacterium that occurs naturally yet sparsely in many soils. When caterpillars and other soft-bodied insects ingest Bt, it makes them sick and ruptures their guts; they stop feeding and die. Several strains are available for specific pests.

The most common form of Bt, Bt *kurstaki* (BTK), is effective against most leaf-eating caterpillars, including cabbageworms, leaf rollers, tomato hornworms, and many others. It is available as a dust, a wettable powder, or a liquid that is mixed with water. Follow package directions and apply to plants when the pests are feeding. To maintain its effectiveness, reapply after heavy rains.

The Safe Way to Spray

Whether you are using an aromatic herbal infusion, dormant oil, or a botanical insecticide, handle yourself and your bug deterrent with care. Consider the following guidelines when making plans to spray:

▲ **Wait for settled weather with little wind and no rain.** Too much wind will keep you from getting the substance where you want it. Imminent rain will wash off the agent before it has a chance to do its job.

▲ **Dress yourself well.** When using Bt or natural pesticides, wear long sleeves and rubber gloves, and make sure to follow package directions for mixing the product exactly. Mix only as much as you need. Homemade hot pepper sprays also need to be handled with care. A hand-held pump spray bottle can be used for many small jobs.

▲ **Strain and strain again.** Herbal teas, garlic brews, and other homemade remedies must be strained through cloth at least once or twice if you plan to apply them with a pump spray bottle or pressure sprayer. Otherwise, small particles may clog up the nozzle of the sprayer.

▲ **Use enough to get excellent coverage.** With herbal brews, you may get the best coverage by using a watering can to drench plants.

▲ **If you suffer from allergies, wear a dust mask when handling any powdery substance.** Even if you don't have allergies, wear a mask when handling rotenone or sabadilla.

Bt *san diego* (BTSD) is a special strain that controls young larvae of the Colorado potato beetle. Apply to potato leaves as soon as the insect is observed feeding.

Bt *israelensis* (BTI) is not used in the garden, but rather in still-water ponds where mosquitoes breed. When properly used, it kills mosquito larvae (wigglers) before they can become adults.

All Bt products are safe, but you should wear rubber gloves to keep the bacteria from entering any small cuts you may have on your hands. Also avoid splashing Bt in your eyes. Bt loses its effectiveness rapidly after it is mixed with water, so prepare small batches and dispose of any leftover solution by pouring it out on the ground.

Barrier Bands

Insects that crawl up the trunks of trees may be deterred or trapped by bands fastened around tree trunks. You can be creative, using this method to trap cankerworms, codling moths, and various small caterpillars as they travel upward toward the leaves of your fruit trees or downward to pupate. Materials that may stop the pests include strips of cotton batting tied with string, three or four strips of corrugated cardboard tied with wire, or bands of paper covered with a sticky substance (see **Sticky Traps,** page 127). Timing is important when using barrier bands, for they must be installed before the pests are expected and should be removed and destroyed when their job is done. The best time to try tree bands is in late summer to fall, when pests are looking for protected places to overwinter, and mid-spring, when pests emerge.

Boric Acid

A white crystalline powder available at drugstores, boric acid is a potent stomach poison for many insects. It is not appropriate for use in the garden, as it will kill any helpful insect that happens to eat it. But when ants, earwigs, or roaches move inside your house, boric acid will usually take care of the problem.

The challenge is getting the pests to eat it. They are not inclined to eat plain boric acid, but if you mix the powder with something they do like, you have a highly effective bait.

For ants, try mixing 1 tablespoon of boric acid with ½ cup of jelly. Place the mixture in a couple of shallow dishes where ants will find it. Any ants that eat the bait will die.

To rid your kitchen of earwigs and roaches, mix together the following ingredients to make boric acid cookies: ½ cup of boric acid; ¼ cup of sugar; 2 tablespoons of shortening; 1 small onion, finely chopped; ½ cup of flour or cornmeal. Add sufficient water to make the mixture soft enough to roll into little balls. Place the balls where the insects hide. They will be attracted by the smell of the onion and the taste of the sugar and shortening.

If you have small children or dogs, be sure to place the "cookies" where the little ones will not be tempted to taste them. A few drops of blue food coloring may be added to make them look less edible from a human point of view.

Bt

See **Bacillus thuringiensis.**

Chickens: Bantam Hens and Egg-Layers

A few bantam hens provide not only an ornament to any garden but a lively and vigilant crew of animated insect-eaters. With the customary visual keenness of birds, bantams will spot an almost invisible insect and nab it that instant. They are independent and more aware of the ways of the world than most chickens bred for egg production, and they require modest housing and a minimum of feed. In return, they will spend hours every day policing the garden and grounds looking for insects.

The problem with bantams is that they also like some garden crops, especially strawberries, green tomatoes, and young seedlings. Many gardeners restrain their birds during the height of the gardening season, letting them roam and clean the garden of insects only during spring and fall, when they cannot do much damage. Movable pens also may be used to put these fowl to work in specific places where pest problems have been severe.

Even when egg-laying chickens (bigger than bantams) are kept in a pen near the garden, they can be important allies when battling insect pests. Dump bug-ridden plants in a chicken yard, and the chickens will quickly scratch them clean.

Collars

Whereas bands fit snugly around tree trunks, collars are comparatively loose protective devices that may be made from paper, cardboard, or metal. Like bands, collars form a barrier that pests are unable to cross as they try to access your plants.

Collars to keep cutworms from felling young vegetable plants are easily made from paper cups with the bottom removed or strips of cardboard stapled into a ring. Place these protective rings around tomatoes, peppers, and eggplant at transplanting time, and if necessary around beans during the first two weeks after germination. Push the collars one inch into the soil, leaving another inch of collar showing above ground.

Collars made from copper strips are an excellent defense against slugs and snails, which turn around and retreat when they encounter copper. You will need long pieces three to four inches wide, for narrow strips are ineffective. Where slug problems are chronic and severe, as in a strawberry patch, try encircling the bed with copper edging; turn down the edge to form a lip to make it even more difficult for slimy pests to cross. Some garden centers sell thin sheets of copper with a paper backing that can be cut and shaped into collars, or you can buy copper sheeting (flashing) at hardware stores and cut it with tin snips.

Companion Planting

The pest-control method known as companion planting capitalizes on the relationships between plants. The way leaves and roots intermingle can confuse pests in search of host plants, resulting in a reduction in pest problems.

I can give but a few examples of companion schemes that work, since insects and the plants they love vary so much between climates. Generally speaking, marigolds, radishes, and pollen-rich flowers and aromatic herbs make desirable neighbors for garden plants that have numerous insect enemies, such as squash, cucumbers, and cabbage-family crops.

In addition to using companion plants within the same bed or row to repel insects, you can create small plant communities that serve as havens for beneficial insects. A knot of perennial herbs, a hedge or mound of mixed cover-crop plants (for example, annual rye, hairy vetch, and crimson clover), or a cluster of small flowering shrubs placed within the vegetable garden may host numerous mantises, spiders, and other helpful creatures that would have no place to live if you were to clean your garden from edge to edge. For best results, use the space nearest to the beneficial hedge to grow the crops that are the likeliest candidates for insect attack.

After a few seasons, you will probably discover plants that make particularly fine neighbors. Repeat these planting patterns, adding and subtracting plants as you learn more about the relationships they share. Eventually, you may discover companionable "guilds" of plants that show reduced insect problems and improved vigor and productivity of all the members within your unique plant community.

Compost Tea

Compost tea does not kill insects, but it may help control fungal diseases that weaken plants, which in turn may make them more attractive to insects. If you live where mildews and fungal leaf spot diseases are common, you will want to try this easy method for maintaining plant health.

To make the tea, place a shovelful of mature compost in a bucket and add 3 parts water (2 to 3 gallons). Stir well and allow to set for three days. Stir again, strain the mixture through a colander, and then strain it through cloth. It will not smell nice. Pour the tea into a hand-held pump spray bottle or watering can. Thoroughly wet plant leaves by spraying or dousing them with the mixture. The tea's effectiveness will subside after three weeks.

Cultivation

Many pests spend time in the soil as eggs, larvae, or pupae. When you cultivate the soil, they become dislodged and disoriented, and may be eaten by larger predators or killed by weather conditions at the soil's surface. Instead of waiting until spring to work up your garden soil, try to cultivate in fall. Then leave the soil open to the elements for a short time. After a hard freeze or two, cover the soil with a winter mulch to protect it from erosion. In mild winter areas, hardy cover crops or winter vegetables can take the place of mulch.

Darkness

Spider mites, flea beetles, leafhoppers, and other insects that crave warm sunshine may be brought under control by modifying the environment to make it cool and dark. First apply a soapy spray to affected plants, preferably in late afternoon (see **Soap Sprays,** page 126). The next morning, cover plants with a blanket or sheet. Leave cover on for three days, then observe plants after a week. If pest problems continue, repeat the procedure.

Diatomaceous Earth

The fossilized shells and skeletons of a type of ancient algae are mined and packaged as diatomaceous earth. This powder looks like fine clay dust, but the edges of each particle are razor sharp. When soft-bodied insects encounter diatomaceous earth, they suffer numerous small abrasions that often result in death. Diatomaceous earth, often abbreviated as DE, is widely available at garden centers and through mail-order companies. It is different from (and much safer than) the DE used in swimming pool filters.

To control leaf-eating insects, spray plants with water, then dust them with diatomaceous earth while the leaves are wet. When applying it by hand, wear a dust mask to keep from breathing the particles. As long as your air passages are protected, you can apply DE by placing a small amount in a paper bag with several small holes punched in it and shaking it among plant leaves.

You also may lay diatomaceous earth on the soil to discourage slugs, cutworms, and other soft-bodied soil dwellers. When setting out cabbage, broccoli, and other brassicas, a small amount of DE sprinkled into the planting holes will provide some protection against root maggots. Diatomaceous earth is good for the soil, as it contains more than a dozen trace minerals.

Dormant Oil

Gardeners can now choose from several types of horticultural oil that are applied to suffocate hidden pests. The oldest and most common of these is often called dormant oil, since it is applied to woody plants in winter, while they are dormant. If this heavier-weight oil is used when the plants have leaves, the leaves will be damaged.

Dormant oils suffocate many pests that overwinter as eggs or pupae, including scale, leaf rollers, spider mites, aphids, and mealy-bugs. Follow the directions on the package for mixing the product with water, and use a pressure sprayer to apply it. On the day dormant oil is used, temperatures should be well above freezing so that the oil can spread on the twigs as it is supposed to.

In summer, when plants are in leaf, some can be treated with superior oils, which are less threatening to leaf surfaces than heavier dormant oils. Still, before applying any oil to a plant in hot weather, read the label carefully and test the product on a small limb or branch. If leaves remain healthy after several days, you will know it is safe to spray.

Ducks

If chickens are too noisy and nervous for you, consider ducks. They devour insects in huge numbers and don't scratch the soil the way chickens do. However, ducks will eat young plants, ber-ries, and some other garden crops. Bird netting will prevent ducks from damaging plants, or you can keep your ducks in a pen.

Floating Row Covers

Floating row covers are a rather recent invention of the plas-tics industry. They come in many forms, but the most versatile versions for home gardeners are spunbonded floating row covers. These porous, lightweight fabrics resemble interfacing used in sew-ing. When placed over plants, they allow sunlight and water to pass through but restrict the movement of insects. Row covers can be used to keep insects away from the crops they seek or to prevent beneficials from visiting plants that have been treated with a natural insecticide.

Floating row covers have endless uses in the garden. Temperatures beneath row covers are a few degrees warmer than normal, so they can speed the growth of plants in cold weather. If row covers are allowed to chafe against the growing tips of tender plants (such as tomatoes), however, they can interfere with growth. With many crops such as peppers, it is a good idea to lay floating row covers over hoops made of flexible plastic pipe. Or you can plant some corn among the plants to be covered and let the corn hold the row covers aloft.

In addition to letting row covers float over entire beds or rows, you can use a double thickness over cold frames in cool weather. If you allow ducks or other fowl to range in the garden, floating row covers can keep them from plucking up young plants. Wrapping row covers around the outside of tomato cages may keep out thrips and leafhoppers.

Flowers

Like aromatic herbs, some flowers attract beneficial insects and repel those that cause trouble. All flowers are therefore welcome additions to the food garden, where they enhance visual beauty and add diversity to the mix of plants.

A few flowers can be used to make teas and infusions to combat pest problems. Marigolds and calendula blossoms produce a strongly scented tea that may repel aphids and other small insects. Chamomile flowers (often listed among herbs) yield a refreshing tea that old-timers sprayed on seedling beds to prevent damping off.

The best flowers for luring beneficial insects to your garden produce plenty of pollen or nectar. Daisies, sunflowers, and many other flowers fit this description. However, since most flowers bloom for only a few weeks, it may take some brainwork to come up with a landscaping plan that provides a continuous source of pollen and nectar, especially if you live where growing seasons are long.

In addition to cultivated flowers, include wildflowers wherever you can. Many of the best predacious insects are natives and are drawn to native flowering plants such as goldenrod, yarrow, bee balm, Queen Anne's lace, and butterfly weed. The bloom time of each is short, but while they are in bloom they serve as little sanctuaries for many of your most valuable beneficial species. Every August when my wild clematis (virgin's bower) blooms, I get my best look at the many beneficials that inhabit my yard.

Garlic Brew

One of the best all-purpose pest sprays you can make includes 4 to 6 cloves of garlic, 1 small pungent onion, and 2 hot peppers (or 1 teaspoon of ground cayenne pepper). Place these ingredients in a blender with 1 quart of water and blend until liquefied. Allow the brew to sit overnight, then strain it through cloth. Add 3 drops of liquid soap to the mixture as you pour it into a pump spray bottle. Use this brew on pests that are eating plant leaves.

Handpicking

Though not a formula or recipe, handpicking should be your first line of defense against any pests that are large enough and slow enough to gather by hand. When handpicking, take along a jar or can containing vegetable oil, very hot water, or a half-and-half mixture of water and rubbing alcohol. You also can use cold water with a squirt of liquid dishwashing detergent. Cast collected bugs into the container until dead and dispose of them outside the garden.

If bugs are very numerous or tend to fly away as you approach, try using a hand-held vacuum cleaner to gather them. Or spray the plants with water before handpicking to get the bugs moving. You also can try shaking plants gently to rouse bugs from their hiding places. If you are uncomfortable picking up insects with your bare hands, wear surgical gloves (available at medical supply stores) or tight rubber gloves.

Hot Pepper

If you have ever grown a bumper crop of very hot peppers and wondered what to do with them, pest-control preparations may be your answer. Capsaicin, the compound that makes peppers hot, repels many insects and can be especially valuable when used to discourage ants and the flies whose progeny develop into cabbage, onion, and other root-eating maggots.

Since the greatest concentration of capsaicin is around the seed cavity of hot peppers, make pepper powder or flakes from whole peppers, seeds and all. Gather a quantity of hot peppers and dry them until leathery. Then chop them well with a sharp knife and dry them again until crisp. Finally, pulverize them in a blender or food processor. Throughout the process, wear rubber gloves to keep from getting capsaicin on your fingers, as it will burn. Store your dried, pulverized peppers in a tightly covered jar for up to a year.

In the garden, sprinkle hot pepper powder around cabbage seedlings and onion plants or sets when setting them out. If ants invade your kitchen, lace their entry point and chosen route with a trail of hot pepper. You also may use purchased red pepper, but it can be expensive.

When you see aphid colonies that are being tended by ants, try treating them with a hot pepper spray. Place ¼ cup of hot pepper flakes in a small heat-proof container, add 1 pint of very hot water, and allow the pepper tea to steep overnight. Strain the mixture through cloth before spraying it on the aphid colonies. Pour any excess mixture down the entry holes of ant colonies.

Hot Water

Very hot or boiling water will kill any insect that comes into contact with it. After handpicking insects, the easiest way to dispose of them is to dump them into a pail of very hot water. For good measure, a squirt of liquid dishwashing detergent will make the hot water more lethal. I bring water to a boil in a large pot on the stove, place collected insects in a metal bucket, and then pour the water on them.

You also may pour hot water down the entry hole of ant colonies or underground wasp nests. A couple of gallons of boiling water will kill many adults and cook the eggs and larvae.

In spring, before permanent raised beds are filled with growing plants, dousing landscaping timbers with boiling water will kill slugs and termites hiding inside the beds' walls. It also will kill beneficial ground beetles and earthworms, so use this method only if you have a serious slug or termite problem.

Insecticides (Botanical)

See **Pyrethrum, Rotenone, Ryania, Sabadilla.**

Light Traps

Many night-flying moths and beetles are attracted to light. If you want to capture some of them to learn exactly who they are, or if you know you're having problems with Asiatic garden beetles, June beetles, or various moths, rigging up a light trap is quite simple. Start with a medium to large cardboard box. Inside, install a single-bulb light fixture that you can attach to an outdoor-grade extension cord. The light fixture can be an old lamp, a shop light, or a socket purchased at a hardware store. Use a bulb that's 75 watts or less to limit heat buildup within the box, and make sure the bulb sits away from the cardboard.

Before cutting an entry hole in the other side of the box, fashion a funnel out of any flexible sheeting material and staple it together. Roofing tar paper, poster board, or any semirigid plastic, paper, or metal material will do. Make the narrow end of the funnel two to three inches (five to eight cm) in diameter.

When the funnel is finished, make a hole in the top of the box so that the funnel fits into it quite snugly. Assemble the pieces, plug the light into the extension cord, and set the box in the garden on a chair or bench to raise it three or four feet (about one meter) above the ground. Turn on the light an hour after sunset and leave it on for two hours.

It's fine to wait until the next day to examine the bugs inside. To keep the insects from leaving, remove the funnel and cover the entry hole with a small board. If you know you will want to dispose of the bugs you catch, you can refine your trap by attaching stretchy sleeves of old hosiery to the entry hole. When you're ready to empty the trap, you can detach the sleeve, dip it in very hot water for a minute, and then dump out the load.

Lime

The same lime you use to sweeten acidic soil has been hailed as a pest-control remedy for hundreds of years. As the dusting of lime is washed from leaf surfaces by rainfall, it enriches the soil. Try lime to discourage flea beetles on young greens and eggplant. For best results, dust lightly in early morning when plants are wet with dew. A collar of lime laid down around leafy greens or other vegetables discourages slugs, which suffer when they cross a barrier of pure lime. However, rain or water renders such barriers ineffective, so they must be renewed after wetting. Use diatomaceous earth instead of lime around potatoes and strawberries, as lime may raise the soil's pH, and these two like acidic (low-pH) soil.

Milky Spore Disease

Japanese beetles are such a widespread pest in the East that controlling them calls for large-scale effort. If you have a lot of property, you probably have millions of Japanese beetle larvae living a few inches below the soil's surface, munching away on grass and weed roots. Milky spore disease is a bacterial formulation (*Bacillus popilliae*) that kills the grubs as they feed. It also kills the grubs of June beetles. To use it, simply spread the purchased powder or granules over your land just before a rain. You may throw the granules about like grass seed or drop tablespoons of powder on the ground every three or four feet. The bacteria are harmless to earthworms.

If you can cover a wide area (and get your neighbors to treat their land, too), milky spore can have a dramatic impact on Japanese beetle populations. You will still see some beetles, especially during the first two years after treatment. Handpick them or collect them in pheromone traps (see page 120).

Mulch

Mulches are almost always good for plants and often are bad news for bugs. Potatoes grown with a deep straw mulch tend to have few Colorado potato beetles. Wherever deep organic mulches are used, predators such as toads and snakes tend to be more numerous. Organic mulches are a relatively easy way to add organic matter to soil, increasing the health of the soil and thus the health of the plants it supports.

With a few plants, you may find that mulching has little impact on plant vitality or may actually contribute to pest problems. Squash bugs use mulch as a safe haven, and because large squash leaves do a good job of shading the soil, a mulch is of questionable value with this crop. Where slug problems are severe, mulches can make things worse, as they create exactly the type of damp, sheltered habitat that slugs adore.

Various roll-out paper-type mulches are now becoming available that may replace black plastic, which is difficult to reuse and recycle. Where aphids, thrips, and leafhoppers spread viral diseases, different-colored paper mulches sometimes confuse them in their search for host plants; reflective mulches work against aphids on pepper plants.

Neem

Not so long ago, scientists discovered that extracts from the bark and seeds of neem trees (*Azadirachta indica*) have broad-spectrum insecticidal properties. Neem-based commercial products have entered the marketplace, but the Environmental Protection Agency (EPA) has not completed the process in which the new neem pesticides are approved for use on various crops.

Neem causes pests to slow down their feeding but does not instantly kill them. When you use a neem product, mix it according to package directions, and use only on plants listed on the label. If a plant is not listed, but the pest in question is named in relation to another plant, that means the testing process required by government regulations is incomplete.

In coastal states near the Gulf of Mexico, a closely related tree, the chinaberry (*Melia azedarach*), grows in great profusion. My grandmother had one in her Mississippi yard, and we children enjoyed many stinging battles using the chinaberry seeds as ammunition. It turns out that chinaberry seeds, well bruised and soaked in warm water, may yield a potent neemlike insecticide for controlling a number of pests for which rotenone is the usual last resort. Chinaberry tea is well worth trying if you happen to have a chinaberry tree close by.

Nematodes

In warm climates, the word *nematode* causes gardeners to shudder, for root-knot nematodes and other species are among the worst soilborne plant pests. Yet beneficial nematodes (microscopic soil-dwelling worms) are at least as numerous as destructive ones. These organisms can be used to control unusually large populations of cutworms, root maggots, symphylans, and other soft-bodied subterranean pests.

For the best results, apply beneficial nematodes to the soil in late spring during a period of rainy weather. Pay attention to the directions on the package and follow them carefully. Use beneficial nematodes only when you know for sure that a teeming population of nematode prey is present.

Nicotine

Nicotine has been used to control insects for hundreds of years, but I think gardeners are well advised to get along without it. It is extremely toxic to humans and other warm-blooded animals. It can be absorbed through human skin and remains poisonous on plants for weeks after it is applied. Homemade nicotine preparations made from tobacco may carry tobacco mosaic virus, a disfiguring disease of tomatoes and peppers.

Pheromone Traps

All animals are interested in sex. This is the logic behind pheromone traps and lures, which use sex hormones to attract specific pests. If you live in the country, you probably have seen these contraptions in commercial orchards or near the edges of grain or cotton fields. Farmers use them to monitor pest populations so they will know exactly when biological or chemical control measures will do the most good.

In a home garden, however, you should think carefully before filling your yard with insect pheromones. The resident population of insects is already giving off "come hither" signals. The use of lures and traps may magnify that message so much that it becomes grossly exaggerated.

Instead, use sticky traps to monitor pest populations, and resort to pheromone traps only if you have a large crop to protect. Always choose the right lure for the pest you need to control. Traps and lures for gypsy moths, Japanese beetles, apple maggots, and codling moths are widely available.

Predators

Many garden supply catalogs now sell lady beetles, lacewing eggs, trichogramma wasps, praying mantis egg cases, and other common insect predators. Although releasing these insects in your garden may do no harm, it may do little good unless it is done correctly.

The most important factors are temperature and timing. Unless specifically di-

Introducing Beneficials

1. *Plan your releases when the friendly bugs are likely to find plenty of pests in the immediate vicinity. Late spring to early summer is usually the best time. Keep in mind that lady beetles and lacewings are partial to aphids, trichogrammas parasitize insect eggs, and braconids specialize in caterpillar control.*

2. *Keep purchased bugs or eggs at room temperature until you release them but avoid holding them for more than a few days.*

3. *Release the insects or spread the eggs in the morning or evening, not in the middle of a hot day. Wet down the garden thoroughly first in case the new bugs are thirsty.*

4. *When distributing lacewing or other insect eggs, place them on plants that may harbor their preferred foods, such as aphids, thrips, and small caterpillars.*

5. *If flowers are not yet in bloom and nectar is in short supply, provide supplemental food. Mix ½ cup of brewer's yeast, ½ cup of sugar, and 5 cups of water to make a batch of bug food. Dribble this mixture on a few plants around the garden.*

rected otherwise by the information on the package, plan to release predatory insects in late spring or early summer, when days are warm. In this way, you mimic the natural life cycles of most insects, which overwinter as adults or pupae, emerge and lay eggs, and hatch in time to start eating their fellow insects. If you release predators too early, they will find nothing to eat and will quickly forsake your garden for more promising hunting grounds (see box on page 121, Introducing Beneficials).

Pyrethrum

Pyrethrum is among the most potent (and toxic) natural pesticides. For more than one hundred years, gardeners have used pyrethrum flowers (*Chrysanthemum coccineum*, also known as painted daisies) in their struggles to control garden pests. Pyrethrum has very strong knockdown power. Most insects are quickly paralyzed by it, although some recover within a few hours.

To make your own pyrethrum concoction, gather flowers when they are fully open and dry them quickly in a warm, shaded place. When they're fully dehydrated, store them in a tightly sealed container until you need them. Pyrethrum flowers also may be used fresh. Either way, chop them very well with a sharp knife on a surface not used for food preparation. Place 1 cup of minced blossoms in a heat-proof bowl or bucket and add 1 quart of warm (not boiling) water. Allow the mixture to cool, strain it through cloth, and add 2 drops of liquid soap. Spray this mixture on bug-ridden plants. Return after an hour and handpick bugs that appear comatose but not dead.

Ready-to-use products that list pyreth*rum* as the active ingredient are extracted from plants, while pyreth*roids* are synthetic versions. Since pyrethrum is safer for animals than most other pesticides, it is often the killing agent in dusts and dips made to control fleas on cats and dogs and in spray-can insecticides likely to be used indoors. Use all pyrethrum preparations with great restraint in your garden, as they are toxic to lady beetles and other beneficials. On the plus side, these chemicals rapidly degrade in sunlight and do not linger long in the environment.

Radish

The insect-deterrent power of radishes never ceases to amaze me. At first I didn't believe it when fellow gardeners told me that radishes reliably protect cucurbits from cucumber beetles and other pests. Then my own garden proved them right. More recently, I grew two beds of kohlrabi with and without radish companions. Whereas the bed with radishes had not a single cabbageworm, the other had many. In my experience, the greatest protection is realized when radishes are allowed to flower.

Resistant Varieties

Pesky insects are particular about what they will eat, and some show definite preferences for certain varieties. Cucumber beetles like most American cucumbers, which carry a gene for bitterness that encourages their feeding, and tend to stay away from oriental cukes, which lack the bitterness gene. Modern varieties described as nonbitter are naturally resistant to cucumber-beetle feeding.

Several other crops resist certain insects. Squash vine borers will sabotage any variety classified as *Cucurbita pepo*, which includes all summer squash, pumpkins, and several types of winter squash, but seldom damage butternuts (which are a different species, *C. moschata*).

Every year, new varieties are released that show better pest resistance than older ones. You can now plant carrots that resist rust fly, sweet potatoes that resist several insects, and tomatoes that resist nematodes. In a few years, you may be able to grow potatoes that are naturally resistant to Colorado potato beetles.

In your own garden, you may notice that some varieties escape insect damage even though no claims of resistance are made in seed catalogs. Keep track of these varieties. Corn with tight husks and beans with thick pod walls can provide so much physical restriction to insect feeding that the result is improved pest tolerance.

Rogueing

In horticultural jargon, rogueing means pulling out plants that are suffering from a pest or disease or that exhibit strange symptoms of genetic abnormality. Rogueing for pest-control purposes is a simple matter of getting rid of the most susceptible specimens to reduce possible threats to neighboring plants. Because healthy plants are better able to resist insect challenges than sickly ones, rogueing out the weaklings can contribute to the overall health of your garden.

I often rogue out squash plants that appear to be magnets for insects, as well as individual bush beans that have so many Mexican bean beetle larvae that handpicking them is not feasible. When plants are crowded, pulling up those that have the most insects removes many unwanted pests and improves the growing conditions for the plants left behind.

When pulling up plants that are loaded with insects, either swoop them quickly into a wheelbarrow or cart or spread an old sheet over them before you pull the plants. If you work too slowly, the insects may have time to escape and return to the scene of the crime. For the same reason, don't simply toss the infested plants on top of a compost pile.

Rotenone, Derris

If you go to a garden center and ask for a natural all-purpose pesticide, you will be handed a box or bag of rotenone. Made from any of several different tropical plants (including several species of *Derris* and *Lonchocarpus*), rotenone is a potent insecticide that should be handled very carefully. It is toxic to beneficial insects, fish, and frogs. In fact, when fish ponds are cleaned prior to restocking, rotenone is the fish killer of choice. It remains active in the environment for a week or slightly longer.

Rotenone can be used in a positive way when other remedies have been exhausted. You may use it to treat very severely infested plants, then cover them with floating row covers for five days to keep beneficial insects from entering the treated area. When applying rotenone, do not breathe the dust or spray, and avoid getting it on your skin. Use rotenone only on plants that will not be eaten within a week.

Ryania

Like rotenone, ryania is a natural pesticide made from a tropical plant (*Ryania speciosa*). It will kill almost any insect that comes into contact with it, as well as beneficial insects and fish. Before you consider ryania, try less toxic substances such as Bt (for leaf-eating caterpillars) or sabadilla (for beetles). If you do decide that ryania is needed, follow package directions exactly and wear rubber gloves and protective clothing to avoid breathing it or getting it on your skin. Cover plants with floating row covers after treatment with ryania to keep beneficials from entering the treated area. Unless you grow fruits or vegetables commercially, you will probably never need this potent insecticide.

Sabadilla

This natural pesticide, derived from a South American lily (*Schoenocaulon officinale*), fell out of favor when synthetic pesticides came into use. However, it has come back on the market and may be the potent pesticide of choice for home gardeners. On the plus side, sabadilla retains its potency for many years, so if you want to keep a strong pesticide on hand for emergencies, you can trust it to remain effective when kept in a cool, dark place. Sabadilla is normally sold as a dust mixed with fine clay. It is highly effective when used to control most beetles that eat plant leaves — the same pests that Bt cannot control.

Pay Attention to Pesticide Labels

Pesticides of all types — biological, natural, and synthetic — carry important information about appropriate use on their labels. They are not registered for use against certain insects but rather for use on certain plants. Legally, you can use them only on the plants listed on the label.

The label will also tell you how to store the pesticide. A high shelf in a cool, dark closet is usually best. Always store pesticides in their original containers, and reread the labels every time you use them.

On the negative side, sabadilla will make you sneeze if you breathe even a wisp of it. (It was long used by huckster medicine men as sneeze powder!) Also, sabadilla also can harm beneficials and honeybees, so use it wisely and with restraint. For the best results, sprinkle the dust on damp leaves to control squash bugs, cucumber beetles, Japanese beetles, and grasshoppers. It is approved for use on most edible crops and can be applied to any flower or ornamental. Sabadilla breaks down rapidly when exposed to sunlight, but you will probably want to wait a week before eating plants treated with it.

Soap

The fatty acids in soap are bad news for many small insects such as aphids, thrips, mites, and whiteflies. When soap is applied to the insects' bodies, it penetrates their "skin" and often causes them to rupture and die. When using soap to control problem insects, it is important to get the spray directly on the pests. (Coat the undersides as well as the tops of leaves.) Few insects are harmed by eating small amounts of soap.

Commercial insecticidal soaps are specially created for use against insects, and they are inexpensive and easy to use. You also can make your own soap spray by mixing 1 teaspoon of liquid soap (or dishwashing detergent) with 1 quart of water. Either type of soap (and especially dishwashing detergent) can harm some plant leaves, so always test your soap spray on a few leaves before wetting down an entire crop. In general, plants with thick leaves, such as members of the cabbage family, accept soap spray very well; thin-leafed beans or peas may suffer slight burns.

When using homemade sprays made from herbs, garlic, or hot peppers, a few drops of soap added to the mixture will help the spray spread and stick to plant leaves. For spider mites on delicate impatiens, I have used a spray made from orange peels steeped in boiling water, with a few drops of soap added after the mixture cooled. Whenever you use soap, use only a little to reduce the possibility of leaf injury. Sprays in which the active ingredient is soap should be much soapier than remedies in which drops of soap are used as a surfactant.

Sticky Traps

Whether you are learning to identify insects in your garden, monitoring populations of unwanted guests, or mounting a strong defense against a pest gone out of control, sticky traps are among a gardener's most useful tools. The traps themselves can be home-made (a fun project in itself), but you will probably want to buy the sticky stuff that snares bugs that alight on it. Two widely available products — Tanglefoot and Tangle-Trap — are specially made for this purpose. Simply smear them on your traps, and you can study, count, and dispose of the bugs you capture.

Determined do-it-yourselfers can make their own sticky stuff, but the main ingredient — resin — is hard to come by. If you mix together equal parts resin, castor oil, and turpentine, you will have a nasty sticky mixture to spread on your traps.

As for the traps, think about the pests you want to capture and fashion an attractive device for catching them. For example, traps painted the same yellow-orange color as cucurbit flowers may entice cucumber beetles to investigate them. Coat the inside of a small yellow bowl (such as a soft margarine tub) with Tangle-Trap, and place some cucumber peelings or a cantaloupe rind in the bottom. Set the trap among cucurbit vines, and within a day you will know whether cucumber beetles are present.

In a similar way, make fake apples from circles of wood, paint them red, cover them with stickum, and hang them in your apple trees in early summer to capture the flies whose eggs hatch into apple maggots.

Sticky traps are most useful against fast-moving pests that fly. Sticky pieces of cardboard dangling above potatoes may trap potato leafhoppers. Aphids, whiteflies, leaf-miner flies, and other tiny winged creatures also are easy to catch in sticky traps. Yellow cards precoated with Tangle-Trap are available for people who don't like the mess of making their own.

Tansy

As an aromatic herb, tansy can be used in teas to discourage cabbage-family pests. The leaves are very pungent, and rubbing them into a dog's fur may repel fleas, just as bruising them on your clothes may make you less attractive to mosquitoes. The flavor of tansy is so strong that you may find few culinary uses for it, but as a member of your garden's plant community, it commands great respect. The small, pollen-rich flowers are much sought after by beneficial wasps and flies, and its aroma may confuse or repel pests in search of host plants.

Tansy is a vigorous perennial that likes to spread, so choose its location carefully. An outside edge of the garden that is mowed on all sides is a good choice, or you may place it alongside mint between a brick wall and a mowed area. Should you need to plant it within a garden bed, plant it in a large container and sink the container in the ground to its rim. If left to grow unrestricted, tansy becomes invasive, and you will be constantly digging it out from places where you want to grow other things.

Timed Plantings

Many insects emerge and look for host plants at specific times. Frequently you can help your crops escape serious damage by planting them either earlier or later than pests expect to find them. For example, the assorted pests that infest sweet corn are generally less severe on early crops. Bean beetles on bush beans and flea beetles on leafy greens are often much more formidable in the spring than in the fall.

To make the most of timed plantings in your garden, keep records of when your worst insect enemies appear as well as planting times that seem to work especially well. After a few seasons, these records can give you important information on when to plant your most pest-free garden ever.

Trap Crops

The logic behind trap crops goes like this: plant something that a common pest likes a lot, and they will be so attracted to that plant (the trap crop) that they will leave other plants alone. This method can work well when carefully used, but you always run the risk of attracting some insects who might not show up if you didn't plant the trap crop in the first place.

Some examples of the trap-crop technique include sowing turnip greens to trap harlequin bugs hanging around in late summer, growing arugula or radishes to lure flea beetles away from other spring greens, planting zucchini ahead of other summer squash to attract squash bugs, or growing bush beans before pole beans so the bush beans bear the brunt of early Mexican bean beetle infestation.

In my garden I find that accidental trap crops are better than the ones I plant on purpose. When I see insects all over a certain species (or variety), I may decide right then that it's a trap crop. To get it out of the garden, I throw an old sheet over the plant, pull it up, and quickly remove it from the garden, bugs and all.

Vegetable Baits

You can capture several pests by using vegetable or fruit baits. The logic is simple: attract pests with something they like, then gather them up before they can escape.

To lure and capture wireworms (see page 101), take several large metal cans, such as coffee cans, and use nails to punch numerous holes in the sides. Fill the cans half full with cut-up potatoes (use blemished or sprouting ones). Bury the cans near potatoes or carrots so that the tops are barely visible. Cover the tops with a small board covered with some mulch. Check the traps twice a week and dispose of trapped wireworms and old bait. Carrots also may be used as bait.

To lure cucumber beetles away from growing plants, set bowls or plates of cantaloupe and cucumber rinds in the garden on a warm morning. When a number of beetles have assembled on the baits, quickly swoop down and capture them in a butterfly net. Empty the net into a pail of very hot soapy water.

Grapefruit and cantaloupe rinds can be used to lure slugs, snails, and pill bugs. Invert the rinds on the ground in the evening, then go out first thing in the morning to collect the prisoners.

You can lure many other pests by setting out caches of attractive foods. Observe which pests are eating in the garden, then use vegetable and fruit trimmings destined for the compost heap to lure them.

Wood Ashes

Wood ashes make a valuable soil amendment because of their potash content, but they also can be used as first aid against several pests. Wood ashes sprinkled around onions and cabbage may discourage the flies whose babies are root maggots. Squash bugs are easier to spot when dusted with wood ashes, and the ashes do not harm plant leaves. Gather wood ashes from your fireplace in winter and keep them in a dry, closed container until you need them. Do not substitute coal or any other type of ashes for wood ashes.

Appendix A
Sources for Natural
Pest-Control Products

Garden centers and general mail-order seed companies sell many of the products described in Chapter 5. However, if you have trouble finding natural pest-control products, check with the following specialty mail-order companies.

A-1 Unique Insect Control
916-961-7945
www.a-1unique.com

Beneficial Insectary, Inc.
800-477-3715
www.insectary.com

Bonide Products, Inc.
www.bonide.com

Bountiful Gardens
707-459-6410
www.bountifulgardens.org

CedarCide.com
800-842-1464
www.cedarcide.com

Contech Enterprises, Inc.
800-767-8658
www.contech-inc.com

Dr T's Nature Products
800-800-1819
www.drtsnatureproducts.com

Extremely Green Gardening Company
781-878-5397
www.extremelygreen.com

Gardener's Supply Company
888-833-1412
www.gardeners.com

Gardens Alive! Inc.
513-354-1482
www.gardensalive.com

Great Lakes IPM Inc.
800-235-0285
www.greatlakesipm.com

Harmony Farm Supply & Nursery
707-823-9125
www.harmonyfarm.com

Irish Eyes Garden Seeds
509-933-7150
www.irisheyesgardenseeds.com

Natural Insect Control
905-382-2904
www.naturalinsectcontrol.com

Nature's Control
541-245-6033
www.naturescontrol.com

Ohio Earth Food, Inc.
330-877-9356
www.ohioearthfood.com

Peaceful Valley Farm Supply, Inc.
888-784-1722
www.groworganic.com

Planet Natural
800-289-6656
www.planetnatural.com

Richters Herbs
905-640-6677
www.richters.com

Seabright Laboratories
800-284-7363
www.seabrightlabs.com

St. Gabriel Organics
Formerly St. Gabriel Laboratories
800-801-0061
www.stgl.us

Woodstream Corporation
800-800-1819
www.saferbrand.com

APPENDIX B
Scientific Names of Common Garden Insects

In research papers, pests are often identified only by their scientific names. Also, common names differ from place to place. Students who wish to pursue the study of insects and other pests may use the following scientific names for a starting point in their inquiry.

Ant — numerous species within the family Formacidae
Aphid — hundreds of species in the family Aphididae
Armyworm — true armyworm: *Pseudaletia unipuncta*
    fall armyworm: *Spodoptera frugiperda*
Asiatic garden beetle — *Maladera castanea*
Asparagus beetle — *Crioceris asparagi*
Assassin bug — numerous species of the family Reduviidae, including the wheelbug, *Arilus cristatus*
Blister beetle — several species in the family Meloidae
Borers — many are members of the family Sesiidae (clearwing moths)
Braconid wasp — many species of the family Braconidae, including *Apanteles congregatus* (on tomato hornworm), *Lysiphlebus testaceipes* (on aphid), and *Macrocentrus ancylivorus* (on codling moth)
Cabbage root maggot — *Delia brassicae* (formerly *Hylema brassicae*)
Cabbageworm — *Pieris rapae*

Cabbage looper — *Trichoplusia ni*

Cankerworm — spring: *Paleacrita vernata*
fall: *Alsophila pometaria*

Carrot rust fly — *Psila rosae*

Caterpillar — larvae of all moths and butterflies (order Lepidoptera)

Codling moth — *Cydia pomonella*

Colorado potato beetle — *Leptinotarsa decemlineata*

Corn earworm — *Heliothis zea*

Cucumber beetle — striped: *Acalymma* species
spotted: *Diabrotica* species

Cutworm — larvae of many moths belonging to the family Noctuidae, including *Agrotis* and *Nephelodes* species

Dragonfly — numerous members of the order Odonata

Earthworm — numerous members of the family Lumbricidae (phylum Annelida)

Earwig — *Forficula auricularia*

European corn borer — *Ostrinia nubilalis*

Fall webworm — *Hyphantria cunea*

Firefly — many species, including *Photinus*, *Lamprorhiza*, and *Photuris*

Flea beetle — several species, including *Epitrix* species, *Phyllotreta* species, and others in the family Chrysomelidae

Four-lined plant bug — *Poecilocapsus lineatus*

Fruit flies — several *Rhagoletis* species, including *R. pomonella* (apple maggot), *R. mendax* (blueberry maggot), and *R. cingulata* (cherry maggot)

Grasshopper — numerous species of the family Acrididae

Ground beetle — numerous species of the family Carabidae

Grub — larvae of numerous beetles in the family Scarabaeidae

Gypsy moth — *Lymantria dispar*

Harlequin bug — *Murgantia histrionica*

Honeybee — *Apis mellifera*

Hornworm (tomato) — *Manduca quinquemaculata*

Ichneumon wasp — huge group of species belonging to the family Ichneumonidae

Japanese beetle — *Popillia japonica*

June beetle — up to 100 slightly different species of *Phyllophaga* or *Lachnosterna*

Lacewing — several species of *Chrysopa*

Lady beetle — several species of *Hippodamia* and *Chilocorus* (family Coccinelidae)

Leafhopper — *Empoasca fabae* (potato leafhopper) and many members of the family Cicadellidae

Leaf miner — species of the family Agromyzidae (order Diptera — flies); also species in the order Lepidoptera (butterflies) and some Coleoptera (beetles)

Leaf roller — *Archips argyrospila*

Mealybug — various species in the family Pseudococcidae

Mexican bean beetle — *Epilachna varivestis*

Mosquito — numerous members of the family Culicidae

Nematode — various members of the phylum Nematoda, including root-knot nematodes (genus *Meliodogyne*), cyst nematodes (genus *Heterodera*), and several others

Onion maggot — *Delia antiqua*

Parsley worm — *Papilio polyxenes*

Pear psylla — *Cacopsylla pyricola*

Pill bug — crustaceans of the suborder Oniscoidea

Plum curculio — *Conotrachelus nenuphar*

Praying mantis — *Stagmomantis carolina*, *Tenodera aridifolia sinensis*, and *Mantis religiosa*

Raspberry cane borer — *Agrilus ruficollis* and *Oberea bimaculata*

Robber fly — many species in the family Asilidae, including *Erax maculata*

Rose chafer — several species of *Macrodactylus*

Scale — numerous species of the family Coccidae (soft scales) and Diaspididae (armored scales)

Slug — about 30 species in the phylum Mollusca, including *Limax maximus* (spotted garden slug) and *Agriolimax reticulatus* (gray garden slug)

Snail — up to 100 species in the phylum Mollusca, including *Helix aspersa* (brown garden snail)

Soldier beetle — *Chauliognathus pennsylvanicus* and *Podabrus tomentosus*

Soldier bug — several species of *Podisus*, including *P. maculiventris*

Spider — thousands of species within the order Araneae

Spider mite — *Tetranychus urticae*

Squash borer — *Melittia cucurbitae*

Squash bug — *Anasa tristis*

Symphylan — *Scutigerella immaculata*

Syrphid fly — many species in the family Syrphidae, including *Didea fasciata*

Tachinid fly — many species belonging to the family Tachinidae, including *Trichopoda pennipes*

Tarnished plant bug — *Lygus lineolaris* and other *Lygus* species

Tent caterpillar — *Malacosoma americanum*

Termite — several species of *Reticulitermes*, *Incisitermes*, and *Coptotermes*

Thrips — several species of the family Thripidae, including *Thrips tabaci* (onion thrips)

Trichogramma wasp — *Trichogramma minutum* and other species

Wasp — several species of *Polistes* (paper wasps) and *Vespula* (yellow jackets and others)

Weevil — numerous species, including *Acanthoscelides* (bean weevil) and *Callosobruchus* (cowpea weevil)

Whitefly — numerous members of the family Aleyrodidae, including *Trialeurodes vaporariorum* and citrus whiteflies *Dialeurodes citrifolii* and *Aleurothrixus floccosus*

Wireworm — several *Limonius* species and others of the family Elateridae

APPENDIX C
Basic Equivalents for U.S./Metric Measurements

	U.S.	Metric
Volume		
	1 teaspoon	5 ml
	1 tablespoon	15 ml
	2 tablespoons	30 ml
	¼ cup	70 ml
	½ cup	140 ml
	1 cup	280 ml
	4 cups	1 liter (approximate)
	1 pint	500 ml (approximate)
	1 quart	1.1 liters
	1 gallon	3.8 liters
Weight		
	1 ounce	28 g
	1 pound	454 g
	2.2 pounds	1 kg
Length		
	¼ inch	6 mm
	1 inch	2.54 cm
	1 foot	30.5 cm

INDEX

(Illustrations are indicated by page numbers in *italics*.)

Trichogramma wasps, *97*, 97
True bugs, 6
Turnip, 30, 57, 64

V
Vacuum cleaner, 115
Vegetable baits, 129
Viral diseases, 13
Virgin's bower, 115

W
Wasps, 65, 98, 94–99, 116
Water, hot, 116–17
Weevils, *99*, 99–100
Wheel bug, 40

Whiteflies, *100*, 100, 126, 127
Wildflowers, 114–15
Winter squash, 29–30, 90–91
Wireworms, *101*, 101, 129
Wood ashes, 130
Wood louse. *See* Pill bug
Wormwood, 60, 105, 106

Y
Yarrow, 115
Yellow jacket wasps, 65, 98–99

Z
Zucchini, 90